An Introduction
to
Applied Professional Research
for Accountants

An Introduction
to
Applied Professional Research
for Accountants

David A. Ziebart
University of Ilinois at Urbana—Champaign

Contributing Authors:

Anita L. Feller
University of Illinois at Urbana—Champaign

Karen H. Molloy
University of Illinois at Urbana—Champaign

Thomas C. Omer
University of Illinois at Chicago

 PRENTICE HALL, Upper Saddle River, New Jersey 07458

Editor-in-Chief: *P.J. Boardman*
Production Editor: *Lynda Paolucci*
Manufacturing Buyer: *Lisa DiMaulo*
Senior Manufacturing Supervisor: *Paul Smolenski*
Production Coordinator: *Cindy Spreder*
Cover Designer: *Lorraine Castellano*

© 1998 by Prentice Hall, Inc.
A Simon & Schuster Company
Upper Saddle River, NJ 07458

Library of Congress Cataloging-in-Publication Data
An Introduction to Applied Professional Research for Accountants /
   David A. Ziebart; contributing authors, Anita L. Feller, Karen H.
Molloy, Thomas C. Omer.
         p.   cm.
   ISBN 0-13-755233-5 (alk. paper)
      1. Accounting—Research—Methodology.   I. Ziebart, David Allen.
HF5630.I66   1998
657'.07'2—dc21   97-45201
                                                                 CIP

This book contains materials from authoritative literature of the Financial Accounting Standards Board and the American Institute of Certified Public Accountants. Screen captures of the *Financial Accounting Research System*™ are used with the permission of the Financial Accounting Foundation and Folio Corporation. Screen captures of the RIA OnPoint System are used with the permission of Research Institute of America and Folio Corporation.

The Financial Accounting Research System™ (FARS) is copyrighted by the Financial Accounting Standards Board, 401 Merritt 7, Norwalk, Connecticut 06856. Images from FARS as included in this work have been reproduced with the permission of the Financial Accounting Standards Board (FASB). Descriptions of FARS as included in this work were created by the authors. The FASB is not responsible for any descriptions or representations of FARS used in this work.

Materials from the RIA OnPoint System are reprinted with permission from Research Institute of America, 90 Fifth Avenue, New York, NY 10011. All rights reserved. For information about RIA Group services, call (800) 431-9025, extension 4.

Exhibit 4-2 is reprinted with permission from ARB 43, Copyright ©1996 American Institute of Certified Public Accountants, Inc.

Prentice-Hall International (UK) Limited, *London*
Prentice-Hall of Australia Pty. Limited, *Sydney*
Prentice-Hall Canada Inc., *Toronto*
Prentice-Hall Hispanoamericana, S.A., *Mexico*
Prentice-Hall of India Private Limited, *New Delhi*
Prentice-Hall of Japan, Inc., *Tokyo*
Simon & Schuster Asia Pte. Ltd., *Singapore*
Editora Prentice-Hall do Brasil, Ltda., *Rio de Janiero*

Printed in the United States of America

10   9   8   7   6   5   4   3   2   1

ISBN 0-13-755233-5

Contents

> "Who does nothing, makes no mistakes;
> who makes no mistakes learns nothing"
>
> Frater Lucas de Burgo Sancti Sepulchri,
> (Lucas Pacioli)
> Ordinis Minorum et Sacre Theologie Magister,
> in arte arithmetice et geometrie.
> *Summa de Arithemetica, Geometria,*
> *Proportioni et Proportionalita*
> Venice 1494

Preface

From my view, the profession of accountancy is changing quickly. This change involves moving to an educational process that includes developing professional skills of problem solving, communicating, and conducting applied professional research. I have been very fortunate to have been involved in the Project Discovery curriculum project, funded by the Accounting Education Change Commission, at the University of Illinois at Urbana-Champaign. This text represents what I have learned from trying to teach students the applied research process and part of my contribution to this change in accountancy education.

In learning to educate students to conduct applied professional research, I discovered that throwing students at the electronic databases was futile. Without a strong systematic approach aimed at teaching the applied research process, students got lost in the professional literature and never understood the richness of the applied research process. As my students may attest, my first attempts to incorporate applied professional research were learning experiences for the students as well as for me. I had not really thought much about issues such as transaction complexity or reading level capabilities; I presumed that the applied research process would appear innate and that they needed little real training–provision of some cases and access to the electronic databases would suffice. My thinking has changed profoundly and this book is the result. Consistent with Project Discovery, the approach of this text is hands-on. Students are involved in many exercises (projects) that allow them to discover the challenges and rewards of applied professional research and to learn by doing.

My contributing authors and I have attempted to develop a resource that combines the attributes of a textbook, a workbook, and a casebook. Our intent is to provide a set of materials that allows students to learn the process of applied research, to practice that process, and to prepare for the profession of accountancy better. The first two chapters introduce students to the topic of applied professional research and to the use of the Internet in applied research. Chapter 3 discusses applied research within the financial accounting and reporting domain. Chapter 4 develops students' skills of using electronic literature databases and contains an elaborate tutorial with many hands-on exercises. In Chapter 5, once students have learned the mechanics of navigating the electronic databases, the applied research process is introduced and practiced. In an attempt to develop students' skills of visualizing complex transactions, Chapter 6 stresses students learning to use graphs, charts, and other visual media to represent complex accounting issues and problems. Chapter 7 introduces students to tax research and allows them to use their skills in a new domain with different and more complex authoritative literature. Chapter 8 provides more advanced Internet tools. Since my intent is to stress the research process and to provide ample opportunities for practice, Chapter 9 provides more than 100 simple research cases keyed for use with the common chapters in an intermediate financial accounting textbook.

I intend this text to be versatile. I believe that it can be used as a supplement in a traditional intermediate accounting sequence or as a major component of an innovative course such as found in the Project Discovery curriculum at the University of Illinois at Urbana-Champaign. In addition, a course that focuses primarily on applied professional research could use this resource as a primary text. I also believe that the book lends itself as a supplement to accounting theory courses at both the undergraduate and graduate levels.

It is essential that I acknowledge the assistance of my contributing authors. In the Project Discovery curriculum project at the University of Illinois, Anita Feller was given the difficult responsibility of teaching students how to access and use the professional literature databases. Her enthusiasm, competence, and dedication to educating students are obvious from even a brief review of Chapter 4. Karen Molloy contributes the chapter on tax research. This chapter is based upon the materials she developed and used as part of my Accounting Institutions and Regulation course. Again, a strong dedication to educating accountancy professionals emanates from her materials. To be progressive in preparing students for the future, I realized that training on using Internet resources was essential for my endeavor. To that end, I needed only to look to Tom Omer, who displayed such great enthusiasm for this project from the moment I discussed it with him. To these three, I must say "thank you."

Besides my contributing authors, many, many individuals have affected this project. My academic colleagues, particularly those at the University of Illinois, various accountancy professionals who pushed and encouraged me to "think outside the box," my editorial team at Prentice Hall who took the risk of signing a book based upon a few conversations, and the many students who have allowed me to try to teach the applied professional research process to them have all assisted in various ways to this project. Special thanks are due to Norton Bedford, Larry Tomassini, Ira Solomon, Chris Olsen, Tom Linsmeier, Tom Stober, Sara Tenney, and P.J. Boardman. In addition, Tom Stober, John Simon, John Hassell, Kathy Petroni, Lisa Koonce, Lucille Montondon, and Jeffrey Harkins assisted by reviewing materials for this endeavor.

I must also thank my family for the time taken away from activities they and I would have enjoyed. Without their support and patience, this project would have never been completed.

As you use the text, please send me comments so that the text can be improved. As I have discovered, learning is a process and I have a ways yet to go. Thanks.

DAZ
Urbana, Illinois

An Introduction
to
Applied Professional Research
for Accountants

Chapter 1
Overview and Introduction
to Professional Research

During Sarah's first assignment as an auditor she encounters a client who maintains that they need not capitalize their lease agreement since some third party guarantees the residual value through an insurance arrangement. Is the client correct?

Brian, who provides consulting advice to Amstar, Incorporated, has been asked to provide advice on a potential transaction. Amstar needs to raise a significant amount of working capital very quickly and has approached a financial institution for a large line of credit. At the initial meeting, the bank informed Amstar that since Amstar is already highly levered, it probably would not meet the criteria for obtaining the desired line of credit given its current level of debt. The bank suggested that Amstar consider approaching one of its current debt holders and arranging a debt-for-equity swap. Amstar has asked Brian how to account for such a transaction in conformance with generally accepted accounting principles. In addition, Amstar is concerned that if a gain were to occur from the transaction it would be taxable. Would it be?

Smith and Jones, an auditing firm in Chicago, is considering bidding for an audit engagement with No Risk Products, Incorporated. No Risk Products manufactures and sells personal computer hardware with a guarantee that the computer will be completely compatible with all hardware and software for the life of the product. Smith and Jones is concerned about adding this client to its practice. Is No Risk low risk?

Jane Price recently started her first job with Acme Products, a manufacturer of health-care products. Jane's supervisor has suggested that Acme value its inventory more conservatively by including only direct manufacturing costs – all overhead will be expensed in the period incurred. Jane understands the importance of conservatism to accountants. Is the omission of all overhead from inventory pricing in conformance with generally accepted accounting principles?

These scenarios are examples of the types of situations that practicing accountants encounter regularly. The similarity is that they all require the accountant to use her or his skills conducting applied professional research to resolve the problem or issue.

APPLIED PROFESSIONAL RESEARCH DEFINED

The profession of accounting has changed from an emphasis on financial record keeping, tax reporting conformance, and auditing to an emphasis on the accountant having the technical capabilities for these activities plus being a problem solver. In addition, the amount of technical literature available to the professional accountant to help in these activities has grown to the point that expertise in accounting requires a general understanding of an area combined with the capability to conduct applied professional research.

Professional applied accounting research is an essential skill for the practicing professional. Many accounting professionals find their activities moving to more problem solving that requires the ability to conduct applied professional research.

Applied professional research can be defined by focusing on each of the three words – *applied*, *professional*, and *research*. Let us start with the latter word – *research*. Research, in general, is the process of obtaining information systematically. That process is deliberate and is conducted carefully and with diligence. Usually, research implies an exhaustive search for and collection of information.

For the accounting professional, research is the process of obtaining information from just about any source that will help him or her in defining, understanding, and solving a problem or issue requiring resolution. That information may include:

> facts about the issue or problem itself;
> knowledge about the context in which the issue or problem
> > arises; or
> professional guidance from the authoritative literature for resolving the issue.

For most people, the term *research* invokes a vision of the research scientist in a laboratory surrounded by a myriad of test tubes and scientific equipment. Although that vision represents a valid perception of one type of research, we intend research in the context of the accounting profession to be *applied* research (our second term from above). We might better think of applied research as the discovery and application of information to resolve problems and/or issues that arise within the context of one's profession. Hence, applied research in accounting focuses on the process of obtaining the pertinent facts and information needed to resolve problems or issues that arise as one practices the profession of accountancy.

Our third term, *professional*, is important. We practice applied research on problems that arise within the context of the professional accountant. As such, our applied research focuses on problems and issues that arise within the realm of the accounting profession and are usually resolved by reference to the body of knowledge contained in the professional accounting literature. This professional literature contains professional pronouncements by authoritative bodies such as the Financial Accounting Standards Board and the American Institute of Certified Public Accountants, as well as specific rules and regulations such as found in the Internal Revenue Code. In addition, sources of professional guidance may include court cases, common law, and securities regulations. In applied professional research, the accountant uses all sources of guidance that are available and applicable in resolving the problem or issue.

It is important to note that applied professional research in accounting is a process and its result is a defensible solution to the problem or issue at hand. By process we mean a systematic routine of identifying the problem or issue, specifying alternative plausible solutions, conducting an inquiry into the propriety of the alternatives, evaluating the authoritative literature found, making a choice among the alternatives, and communicating the results. Since the solution must be defensible, the accounting professional must be certain that the search of the professional literature is exhaustive and the reasoning employed in determining the solution is sound.

Applied professional research is a process of problem identification, information search, interpretation, judgment, and communication. Each step in the process is critical to the outcome and the final resolution of the issue. It is important to note that the process may require repeating some steps many times before we obtain a defensible solution.

In the accounting profession, applied research is an integral part of day-to-day activities. These activities might include research on the appropriate way to account for a certain transaction or alternative means to structure a transaction so that it can be recorded in a certain way. Alternatively, applied professional research might involve finding out the appropriate behavior expected of the professional by reference to an ethical code of behavior. In addition, a professional might be required to investigate whether particular techniques have been determined to be appropriate in an attestation or auditing engagement. On the tax dimension, an accountant might be faced with determining whether an item on a tax return has been handled appropriately. In addition, the tax professional might be called upon to assist in structuring a transaction to take advantage of a tax law or regulation. These instances require the accounting professional to practice the applied research process. Once you have mastered this research process, it can be applied across many different accounting issues and specialities.

APPLIED RESEARCH SKILLS

The applied research process requires the professional to use several skills in completing the following steps in the process:

> problem identification and issue articulation;
> development and communication of a problem statement;
> identification of plausible alternative solutions based upon prior knowledge or theory;
> generation of a research strategy, including keyword generation and choice of database
>> or information resources;
> implementation of the research strategy;
> searching, identifying, and locating applicable information;
> analysis and evaluation of the information obtained;

development of a solution;
communication of the research results; and
documentation of the research process.

Since the final product of this process usually consists of some form of written communication to a superior, a client, or a governmental agency, adequate communication skills are essential.

As one can see, the applied professional research process in accounting requires the professional to exercise judgment throughout several steps in the process. This series of steps in the process may seem rather daunting but can be broken down into manageable components. As your research skills grow, these steps will become more familiar and will blend to form the research process. In this text we will treat each step individually, but continuous integration of these steps into the process is the goal. Eventually, the process will become natural to the professional and the steps will blur into a continuous process.

TYPES OF RESEARCH QUESTIONS

As you can imagine in today's business environment, the types of questions or issues that confront the professional accountant are quite varied. However, it is appropriate for you to think of them in terms of the functional domain, the type of issue, and the context (Figure 1-1). We will discuss each of these in more detail.

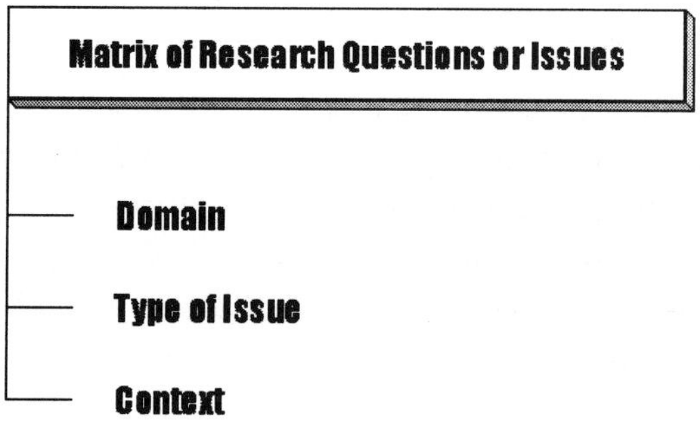

Matrix of Research Questions or Issues

— **Domain**

— **Type of Issue**

— **Context**

FIGURE 1-1

The domain can be thought of as the functional area in accounting in which a problem or issue requiring applied professional research arises. Although the boundaries between domains are fuzzy (and becoming even less clear), it is the domain that provides some guidance about the professional literature that may be brought to bear on the problem. In addition, the domain may constrain the research to a particular area of authoritative literature. Whatever the domain, the research process remains essentially the same. Once you have learned the skill of applied research in one domain, transfer to another domain is easy.

One way to portray the domains is by using traditional functional areas (see Figure 1-2). For instance, financial accounting, cost accounting, taxation, or auditing and attestation are all areas that you may have studied (or may study in the future). Each of these areas has a particular domain of questions or issues that the source of the authoritative literature can separate.   For example, the major authoritative body producing financial accounting guidance is the Financial Accounting Standards Board (FASB). For financial reporting related to publicly traded companies, the Securities and Exchange Commission (SEC) determines the content of the required filings. The taxation area is more complex; Congress, the Internal Revenue Service (IRS), and the court system define the requirements. Standards for conducting auditing and attestation can be found primarily in documents of the American Institute of Certified Public Accountants (AICPA). The Governmental Accounting Standards Board (GASB) sets the standards for governmental accounting, while the Cost Accounting Standards

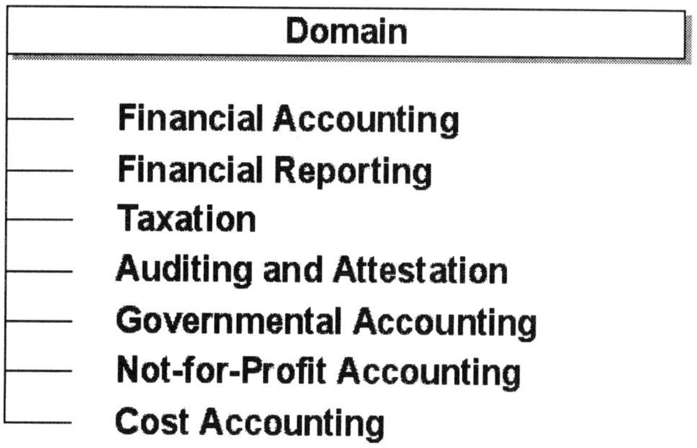

Domain

Financial Accounting
Financial Reporting
Taxation
Auditing and Attestation
Governmental Accounting
Not-for-Profit Accounting
Cost Accounting

FIGURE 1-2

Board (CASB) provides standards in the cost accounting domain. The authoritative literature for not-for-profit accounting is provided by the FASB, as well as audit guides provided by the AICPA and industry practices.

Besides the source of authoritative literature, most applied professional research problems in accounting also can be thought of in terms of the type of issue. Although a problem or issue may contain only a single type of issue, many problems in accounting are actually a combination of types. For our purposes, the three types of questions or issues are "What," "When," and "How." These are illustrated in Figure 1-3.

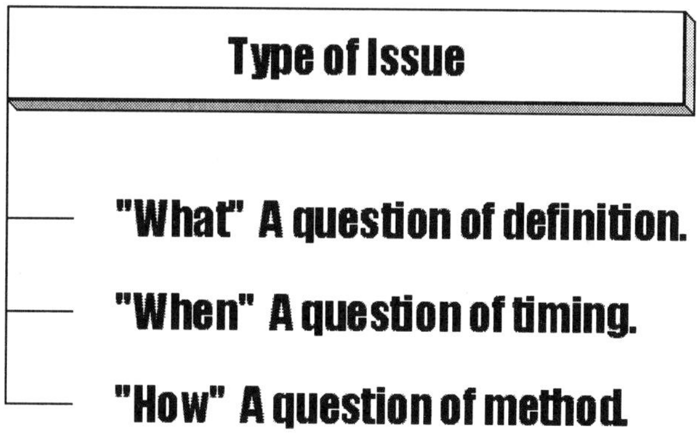

Type of Issue

"What" A question of definition.
"When" A question of timing.
"How" A question of method.

FIGURE 1-3

"What" questions are questions regarding facts or definitions. They usually relate to determining what the facts are for a given issue or situation, or once the facts are determined, applying those facts to decide whether a particular definition applies. Examples of "what" questions include:

Does this lease meet the criteria for capitalization?
Are these assets correctly classified as current assets?
Must inventory include overhead costs?
Is this taxable income?
Are these expenses deductible?
Has our audit been limited to the extent that we must issue a disclaimer of opinion?

Is a not-for-profit organization required to use fund accounting to be in compliance with generally accepted accounting principles?

Must we recognize the liability by "booking" it or can we just disclose it via a footnote?

"When" questions in accountancy are usually questions of timing and focus on determining the point in time some event needs recognition or when a certain professional activity is required. Examples of "when" questions include:

When must a permanent decline in the value of inventory be recognized?

Under the percentage-of-completion method for recognizing revenue, when must a loss be recognized?

During the planning of an audit, when is the client's internal control system considered?

When must a taxpayer file for an extension on a tax return and when is the return then due?

What is the order of events leading up to an initial public offering, and what are the due dates for various filings with the Securities and Exchange Commission?

"How" questions and problems in accounting usually refer to measurement in financial accounting and reporting as well taxation. In auditing and attestation services, "how" usually refers to a specified act that must be undertaken. Examples of "how" questions include:

How is depreciation calculated using a straight-line approach?

How is income measured on long-term construction contracts when the percentage-of-completion method is used?

How are concentrations of risk recognized and disclosed?

How may a taxpayer elect the one-time exclusion of a gain on the sale of a personal residence?

How can analytical review procedures be used in the planning of an attestation engagement?

As can be seen in the prior examples, the questions encountered in professional practice may involve only a single type of question– "what," "when," or "how." However, in many instances requiring applied professional research, the issue or problem may be a combination of multiple questions spanning all three types. For example, does a lease agreement meet the requirements for being capitalized? If so, when is it capitalized? Once capitalized, is depreciation required? When is depreciation expense recognized? How is the lease obligation measured? How is depreciation expense computed?

It is also important to note that the types of problems or issues encountered can be those relating to past transactions or activities. These problems or issues are usually considered of the "compliance" nature. In contrast, some problems or issues are related to the structuring of future transactions or events and are "planning" in nature. For example, in financial reporting, once a lease transaction has been structured and the contract signed, the accountant's role is to decide the correct accounting for the lease transaction. This usually requires determining whether the lease meets the criteria to be capitalized and then applying the professional standards related to capitalized leases. In this situation, the accountant focuses on compliance. However, the accountant could have been asked to determine the means by which we could structure the lease to insure that it would meet the criteria for capitalization. The accountant would then be conducting research of a "planning" nature.

Context

Planning

Compliance

FIGURE 1-4

Much of an accountant's role in assisting a client with taxation is probably misunderstood as assisting with the preparation and filing of the tax return–compliance work. However, in reality, a significant portion of the tax professional's activities involves determining means to reduce taxation on future transactions via tax planning activities.

SOURCES OF INFORMATION IN CONDUCTING APPLIED PROFESSIONAL RESEARCH

Accountants are not constrained to only professional authoritative literature when conducting applied professional research. Instead, accountants, as information professionals, employ whatever information sources are applicable and available to solve the problem. This may include professional literature as well as all sorts of information commonly available in libraries. In addition, information available via the Internet will become ever more important as that resource continues to expand.

While the primary focus of this text is on accessing and using professional literature, the availability of information via Internet sources also must be considered. The key is to realize that the process of conducting applied professional research in accounting can be applied across topical domains (financial reporting, taxation, and auditing) as well as different types of information resources. Once you have learned the process, it is a "tool" to add to your toolkit. Applied research skills are a very important tool that will serve you in many ways in the future.

Chapter 2
Using the Internet
for Applied Research

INTRODUCTION

We have designed this chapter to help you conduct applied research using the Internet. The Internet represents a large and, for most of us, unexplored information storehouse. When you are finished with this chapter, we hope you will find searching this storehouse a much easier task.

There are three objectives to be accomplished in this chapter. First, to guide you in obtaining a "technical proficiency" level that will help you in conducting applied research using Internet resources. Second, to give you strategies for gathering and searching for information using the Internet. Finally, to provide you with examples of information available on the Internet that might be useful in your professional career.

Technical Proficiency

A researcher who engages primarily in applied research must have the technical skills necessary to conduct research in an effective and cost-efficient manner. Because of recent changes in technology, applied research costs can be drastically reduced if the researcher is aware of available tools and, given the tools, is comfortable with their use.

Being a technically proficient applied researcher does not mean that you must be a programmer or systems analyst. After all, you do not have to be a mechanic to drive an automobile, nor a programmer to operate a word processing package or spreadsheet. However, to be a good driver, produce reports, or use a spreadsheet effectively, knowing something about the operating characteristics of the tool you choose to use is necessary. Therefore you will find the chapter full of suggestions about what technical tools can be beneficial and instructions about how to make these tools work for you.

Searching and Search Strategies

One problem with using the Internet as an applied research resource is the overwhelming quantity of information housed at various sites around the world. Researchers can face a daunting task of selecting that information source most relevant to the question they are trying to answer. Most researchers must ask questions such as How do I search for information? Is the information reliable? Is there enough information to answer the question I was asked? Part of this chapter focuses on the search engines available on the Internet. In addition, hints regarding keyword searching, use of search engines, and what to look for in terms of reliability are discussed.

Each search engine has particular features, and your search engine choice may depend on the information you require for answering a specific question or just on personal preferences. Whatever drives your search engine choice, you should use it to your advantage. That means you should have a sense of the database limitations and operating characteristics.

Internet Resources

The Internet is an information paradise. Whatever your information needs, it is likely that some if not all of that information can be found on the Internet. To give you a sense of the depth and breadth of that information, the final section of this chapter provides a summary of the more useful sites for accountants and others engaged in business.

Internet sites are dynamic (change quite often). For example, that information concerning accounting practices in Ireland you bookmarked last week may no longer exist at the same address, and the person responsible for the information may have failed to provide a forwarding address.

APPLIED RESEARCH QUESTIONS AND ANSWERS

Every research project begins with an initial question or problem. In applied research, your supervisor may have already formulated the question you are asked to answer. However, there is no guarantee that the question has been formulated in a manner conducive to gathering or searching for the appropriate information. For example, what if your supervisor or instructor presents you with the following question: "How is this firm doing?" The question is vague. How would you answer it?

How a firm is doing and what information you must acquire to answer the question depends a great deal on how much time you spend developing the precise question to be answered. Answers will depend on whether you want to compare a firm with itself, to other firms in the industry, to other firms in the economy or to some target level of performance. The comparison could also be couched within the U.S. economy or considered as part of a worldwide economic picture. The information sources are different depending on which of these benchmarks you choose to use.

Although the question you are asked to research and answer will be different for each situation, the process of defining the question to answer will enhance your ability to provide answers using the Internet. With the proper tools and a well-defined question, the Internet becomes no more intimidating than your trip to the business library.

INFORMATION ACQUISITION TOOLS

The means for getting information from the Internet involves several types of Internet software. The primary software, the Web browser, which many of you are familiar with, comes in several versions but all work on the same basic principle. The goal for this section is to discuss two popular Web browsers, their differences, and how you can customize a Web browser to enhance your research activities. For times when a Web browser does not meet all your information gathering needs, we discuss alternate software tools.

Web Browsers

As many of you are aware, two Web Browsers are the most popular. They are Netscape from Netscape Communications Corporation and Internet Explorer from Microsoft Corporation. A discussion of each software package and how to optimize its use is provided. The discussion focuses on changing the browser options (Microsoft) or preferences (Netscape) for optimum use.

Microsoft Internet Explorer 3.x

After double clicking on the Internet Explorer icon to start the package, you are presented with a menu bar that includes six menu items: file, edit, view, go, favorites, and help.

File: From this menu item, two selections in the drop-down menu are very important to using the browser, "Save as File" and "Print." The Save as File can be used to save a file being viewed by the browser as an HTML (.html) document or as a "plain text" (.txt). The Print option allows you to send the file being viewed to a local printer. The Save as File option should be used when page content (with proper reference) would enhance a report or presentation. Use of the print option should be minimized because images embedded on the page being viewed are likely to over-whelm the local printer and limit print capabilities for other users on the network.

Edit: From this menu item you can cut or copy selected text from the page being viewed by the browser. The principle is the same as the cut, copy, and paste functions in a word processor.

View: From this menu item two selections, "Source" and "Options," are available in the drop-down menu. Source is useful if information about the page creator (for the page in the browser window) is not obvious. Placing the cursor over the Source selection and clicking once will result in the HTML code that created the page being presented in Microsoft Notepad (a text editor included as part of the Windows operating environment). The document creator's name and corporation may be available between the HTML tags <HEAD> and </HEAD>. Clicking once with your mouse button (left button Windows machines) on the Options selection results in a new dialog box entitled "Options" with six tab markers at the top: general, connection, navigation, programs, security, and advanced. Each of these tabs gives you the means to change browser functions or features. We describe each tab's content; however, detailed discussion will concentrate on the changes available in the tabs marked "general," "navigation," and "programs." The default settings for security, advanced, and connection may be used.

    General: The first tab "General" allows you to select whether sound, image, or video clips should be loaded, and the color of new and visited links. It also provides the means to change the background, and text colors of documents in the browser window, and which toolbars and buttons are available on the main browser window.

Connection: The selections found under this tab marker allow you to change two features of the browser. The first automates the connection to the Internet when dialing into a local network. Placing a checkmark in this box would initiate a dial-up routine whenever Internet Explorer is started. The second feature allows you to identify, if necessary, the proxy server used by the browser when accessing information. A proxy server works on behalf of one or more other servers, usually for screening or firewall purposes. For example, a proxy server may be used in a company to gather all Internet information requests and forward the requests to a server with a direct connection to the Internet. The process is reversed when the direct connection server receives information from the Internet.

Navigation: The "Customize" and "History" sections found under this tab marker allow you to set the Internet address automatically contacted when Internet Explorer is started. Also allowed are changes to the number of days that accessed pages remain in the browser's history file. Internet Explorer's initial installation includes as the default start page Microsoft's home page. To change the default page, either type the site's full HTTP address in the box marked "Address" or access the page with the browser and click once on the button marked "Use Current." To retain the change for future sessions you must click once on the button marked "Apply" and once on the button marked "OK." The History selection allows you to specify how long previously accessed pages should be retained. This is especially helpful if you failed to add an important site to your "Favorites" folder (discussed below). The retention period for pages accessed can be set from zero to 999 days. Two additional options are associated with the History selection, "View History" and "Clear History." The View History button opens a dialog box showing the history of pages accessed by the browser over the retention period. Double clicking on the site icon to left of the History dialog box window takes the user directly to the site indicated. Clicking once on the Clear History button empties the History file. The History file will begin to accumulate addresses with the next page viewed in the browser window.

Programs: The section "Mail and News" allows you to set up the software for receiving e-mail or news group information. The pull-down box for e-mail and news provides a list of software available at your site for these functions. The section "Viewers" allows your browser to deal with a variety of files encountered on the Web. This section allows you to set the file type (extension) and application the browser should open when accessing a file. Many file extensions and applications come preset as part of the Web browser installation package. For example, suppose you access a Web site that has an EXCEL spreadsheet containing summary financial statement data for a firm. Assume that the file has the following fictional name, FINDATA.XLS. How does your browser handle this spreadsheet? The browser's Viewers section has been preset to open the EXCEL application when it encounters a file with the ".xls" extension. Once EXCEL is open, you see and save the spreadsheet for further analysis.

Security: The security tab has three sections: content adviser, certificates, and active content. You are not likely to need to change the preset features. These sections are important if you are the individual responsible for maintaining the quality of information downloaded to your network and the integrity of software downloaded to your machine by Web pages you access.

Advanced: Under this tab you can set reminders about information being transmitted over the Web, temporary Internet files, and several check boxes for advanced features. The temporary Internet files selection is the most important feature under this tab marker. The temporary Internet files area is the cache of Internet Explorer (refer to the definition of cache in the vocabulary section of Chapter 8). It is a portion of your hard drive used to store files viewed during the current session. The size of the storage area is determined as a percentage of your hard drive space. These files are added to the history folder if they differ from previous file requests. Clicking once on the "Settings" button provides you with the ability to determine whether the browser should update the cache files on each visit to the Web site, each time the Web browser is started, or never. Choosing "never" means that no matter what changes have been made to files accessed previously, the Web browser will continue to provide you with the old file until the History time parameter eliminates the file or the cache is emptied (also an option). This probably is not a good choice if you access sites that are often updated. Choosing to update each time the browser is started requires the browser to request from each Web site any new versions of files accessed from the site. This option can be quite time-consuming at start-up but ensures that any new versions of files in the cache from previous browser sessions are available for viewing. Choosing to update each time the Web page is accessed is probably the best option because it limits updating to files currently under consideration.

Go: This menu item provides fast access to various options available on the Web. It provides quick access to the History folder. It also duplicates the back and forward buttons on the browser toolbar. The most important feature here is the ability to go directly to a Web page accessed during a current session without having to use the "back" or "forward" button multiple times. In other words, it is a time saver.

Favorites: This menu item allows Internet sites to be added the browser's memory. You might add to this list because you expect to access information at the site repeatedly. The selections under this menu item are "add to" and "organize" favorites. The organization feature is helpful if you want to collect information sites by topic or source and reduce the time necessary to find information. Clicking once on the "Organize Favorites" selection provides a dialog box for new folder creation or moving Favorites to specific folders. A Favorite can be moved to a folder by selecting the Favorite and dragging it to the folder.

Help: This menu item gives you access to various resources on the Internet. Probably the most helpful selection is the help topics section. Selecting this option brings up a dialog box that provides a keyword searchable index file.

Netscape 3.x (Standard or Gold)

After double clicking on the Netscape icon to start the package you are presented with a menu bar that includes nine menu items: file, edit, view, go, bookmarks, options, directory, window, and help. As with Internet Explorer, we will discuss only the more important items extensively.

File: Depending on your version of Netscape, this menu item will contain many of the same items as Internet Explorer. If you have the Gold version, they include an HTML editor as part of the software so expect more selections to be available. However, like Internet Explorer, two selections on this menu are important for our purposes. They are "Save as" and "Print." The functions for each of these selections are consistent with those described for Internet Explorer.

Edit: See Internet Explorer discussion.

View: This menu item is different from Internet Explorer. Missing from this menu item is "Options," which has been upgraded to a full menu selection in Netscape (see below). Two selections, "Document Source" and "Document Info," are useful from this menu item. Document Source opens an internal or specific Web editor to display the HTML code that created the page. Document Info gives you the Internet address for the text portion of the Web page as well as the address of any page additions such as images, sound files, or video clips. Document Info also indicates when the page was last modified, the file type, and whether there is any security associated with the page. These two features are an extended version of the Source selection found on the View menu item in Internet Explorer and are important for the same reason discussed earlier.

Go: See Internet Explorer discussion for summary of similar options.

Bookmarks: This menu item provides two functions, "Add" and "Go to," bookmarks. These features allow you to add to your select list the Internet sites you feel are important and go directly to those sites. This menu item is more famous than the Internet Explorer Favorites menu item because the Netscape browser was around before Internet Explorer. Bookmarks have become the common reference for sites retained in browser memory for easy return.

Options: This menu item receives full "menu" status in the Netscape browser family. Under this menu option all browser "preferences" can be set to maximize the browser's usefulness. Selections allow you to set security, network, HTML editor, mail and news, and general preferences. Clicking once on these selections produces a tab-oriented window allowing various browser preferences to be set. There are far too many preferences to be discussed fully in this chapter. However, knowing where to set helper applications and other functions for acquiring information will be discussed. Within the "General preferences" selection, two tab markers, "Helper" and "Apps," allow you to set appropriate helper applications and the software you prefer for Telnet access and viewing the source of HTML documents. Like Internet Explorer, the preset extensions and applications should be more than adequate for completing your research project. The Helper tab allows you to determine whether a file should be viewed in the browser window, whether another application should be opened, and whether to ask the user which application should be used to view the file.

Directory, Window, and Help: These three menu items contain selections analogous to those found in Internet Explorer. The differences are not substantial and individual exploration of the options is encouraged.

Web Browser Errors

Whenever you contact a site on the Web, there is the possibility that acquiring the information located there will fail. Problems may occur at the initial contact point or during the process of transferring data. Some problems are related to something that you may have done but can also fix. Others relate to problems on the remote site. The ability to distinguish between a problem you can solve and one you can't eliminates a lot of unnecessary waiting and frustration. We now discuss some errors you might encounter.

DNS Lookup Failed: A DNS Lookup Failed message indicates one of two problems. The first problem might be that the browser could not contact your domain name server. This may occur because the computer housing the server software is offline or the network route to your DNS is down. Neither of these scenarios can you correct. However, if the problem continues, contact your network administrator to report the problem. The second possibility is that the DNS is not aware of the address you are requesting. When a DNS is not aware of an address, it requests address information from a DNS located above it in the Domain Name Hierarchy. Each failure to acquire the appropriate information sends the request to successively higher DNS. When the address cannot be located, an error message is returned to the requestor. This process happens in seconds (microseconds on a good day). The most common cause of this second possibility is that the Web site address is misspelled or typed incorrectly.

File Not Found: This error is very common and is the reason that exclusive reliance on bookmarks or Favorites for information collection is problematic. Web sites are always in a state of change. Web designers, in attempts to improve service, redesign, relocate, and sometimes rename files. Some changes occur because the computer originally chosen to be the Web server cannot efficiently handle the level of information requests and the site is moved to another computer in the same organization. Many sites fail to give users the updated address and therefore the bookmark or Favorite marker you found yesterday returns "File Not Found." The solution for this error type is twofold. First, if you know the domain name of the organization providing the information, you can track the new site by accessing the home page of the organization. Second, competency with search engines will make finding the new site much easier.

Operation Timed Out: This error usually occurs when traffic on the Internet is heavy. Each Web server, to serve information requests efficiently, allocates a number of seconds for an operation to take place (i.e., Web page transfer). When an information request is made the Web client and server interact to make sure that the client receives information packets sent by the server. This involves an error checking routine that ensures that all sent information packets actually arrive. Packet arrival generates a response to or from the client, and to or from the server of packet receipt. When Internet traffic is heavy, responses to and from the server may be slowed by existing traffic and the response to or from the server may not be received in time to complete an operation. When this happens the operation is stopped and you receive an error message indicating a time-out has occurred. When this happens, request the information again or wait until the network traffic load is lighter.

Server Error or Server Busy Error: These errors suggest a problem at the server end of the client/server relationship, not with your browser. The errors mean one of two things: (1) The computer you are trying to access is offline (for service) or has crashed (shut down inexplicably). (2) The computer you are trying to contact is so busy with information requests that the queue for requests is full.

Detecting an Error

Every browser has a status bar at the bottom of the browser window. The status bar indicates where in the process the browser is with regard to the information you requested. If the browser interprets the Web address correctly, the status bar will quickly show that the Web site has been found and the browser is waiting for a reply to the information request. If the status bar shows that the browser is connecting to the numerical IP address for a longer than normal period (a matter of microseconds) rather than showing that the Web site has been found, an error has occurred. Watching this status bar can eliminate unnecessary waiting if you quickly identify that accessing that particular Web site is going to be a problem.

Alternate Information Acquisition Tools

Telnet: Telnet is a user command and an underlying TCP/IP protocol for accessing remote computers. The Web or HTTP protocol and the FTP protocol allow you to request specific files from remote computers, but users are not actually logged on as users of that computer. With Telnet, you log on as a regular user with whatever privileges you may have been granted to the specific applications and data on that computer.

A Telnet command request looks like this (the computer name is made-up). On the command line type the following: telnet the.libraryat.university.edu. The result of this request would be an invitation to log on with a user ID and a prompt for a password. If accepted, you would be logged in like any user who uses this computer every day. Telnet is most likely to be used by program developers and anyone who has a need to use specific applications or data at a particular host computer. Telnet is also the most likely protocol you would use to communicate with the central computer located at your campus or firm.

FTP: FTP (File Transfer Protocol) is the usual way you send files to your server (or receive files from the server). FTP is one of the suite of protocols that are part of TCP/IP. FTP has a user command interface for establishing contact with a server, logging in, and sending, receiving, or otherwise changing files. Many access providers include an FTP utility as part of the setup. Using FTP, you can also update (delete, rename, move, and copy) files at a server that gives you access to these functions. Whether you have these privileges depends on how you log in. Many sites provide anonymous FTP, which restricts user privileges to simply copying files. Home page creators use FTP to transfer files to the directory on a remote Web server where they will be accessed.

Gopher: Gopher is the information structure on Internet servers that preceded the World Wide Web. With access to a server that uses the Gopher protocol, you see a hierarchically structured menu of viewable files.

None of these access utilities is very user-friendly. For Telnet and FTP, the user is required to use the command line normally found on mainframe computers to complete or initiate a login or information transferal. Gopher relies on pull-down menus but is not as user-friendly as your Web browser.

Every computer and telecommunication device has a series of ports. A port is generally a specific place for being physically connected to another device, usually with a socket and plug. Personal computers are provided with one or more serial ports (e.g., modems use serial ports) and usually one parallel port (printers use parallel ports in the Windows environment).

On the Internet, a port is a client specification for contacting a particular service on a server (or daemon). A port is where a server or daemon listens for information requests. There are standard port numbers for many Internet protocols. For example, FTP servers can be accessed at ports 20 and 21, Telnet servers at port 23, and SMTP servers at port 25. By default, the port number for a Web server is 80. You can think of the array of ports as a strip mall with shops designated to provide services to mall visitors. To get the right service you must go to the door of the right store and give the secret code (access routine) to get in. Thus, sending an FTP information request (a port 20 or 21 request) to port 23 (Telnet) goes unanswered. If the server, daemon, or service you require is not available on the machine you are attempting to contact, no one will answer.

You can save time using a Telnet or FTP utility rather than your browser because when your Web browser activates a FTP or Telnet connection it must be coordinated through the Web server operating at port 80. If traffic to the Web server is heavy, the coordination can be slowed to a crawl. Many sites offer users the option to use the FTP or Telnet ports directly. This bypasses the coordination problem that occurs in heavy traffic. The speed difference can be phenomenal. Consequently, being comfortable with all these optional utilities can drastically reduce your information collection time.

Notes:

_____

_____

_____

_____

_____

_____

_____

_____

_____

_____

_____

_____

_____

_____

_____

_____

_____

Exercise 2-1   Name: _____

FTP and Telnet   Section: _____

Instructions: Complete each of the following by accessing the information using Internet resources. Provide the address you used to access the information.

Find a site on the Internet that allows anonymous FTP (be sure to provide the address). Describe the process for logging in and the material available to users who log in.

_____

_____

_____

_____

Source address: _____

Find a site on the Internet that provides Telnet access (be sure to provide the address).

Source address: _____

What information is available at this site?

_____

_____

_____

_____

Source address: _____

Were you able to log in? If not, why not? _____

_____

Exercise 2-2   **Name:** _____
Internet Addresses   **Section:** _____

Instructions: Complete the following by accessing the information using Internet resources.

Explain what service is being provided at the following address. "http://gopher.mtholyoke.edu/."

_____

_____

_____

_____

_____

_____

What organization houses this site? _____

Exercise 2-3   **Name:** _____

Internet Basics   **Section:** _____

Instructions: Complete each of the following by accessing the information using Internet resources. Provide the address you used to access the information.

There are various image formats used on the Internet. One of these formats is called a bitmap image. Using your Web browser, determine the file extension for a bitmap image and indicate how your browser would handle such a file (i.e., what application would be called to view it).

_____

_____

_____

_____

Using your Web browser, determine the size of the cache provided for your browser. Is your browser defined in kilobytes or as a percentage of the computer's hard drive?

_____

_____

What application has been assigned the task of viewing the source of the HTML document in the browser window for your browser?

_____

_____

_____

Notes:

_____

_____

_____

_____

_____

_____

_____

_____

_____

_____

_____

_____

_____

_____

_____

_____

_____

SEARCH ENGINES AND SEARCHING

As the term is generally used, a *search engine* has two parts. The first part is a "robot" or "crawler" that goes to every page or representative pages on the Web and creates a huge index. The second part of a search engine is the interface program that receives your request, compares it with entries in its index, and returns the results to you. Depending on the search engine, the results can be returned with just the link or the link and a short text clip of the information on the page at that link. The abbreviated result allows you to put more links on one page, but the text clip helps identify the information source most relevant to your search.

For most searches, the most popular search engines on the World Wide Web can be found through either:

> Yahoo (http://www.yahoo.com)
> Search.com (http://search.com)
> EasySearcher (http://www.easysearcher.com)

The Yahoo search engine first searches its hierarchically structured subject directory and gives you those entries. Then, it provides a few entries from the AltaVista search engine. It also launches a concurrent search for entries matching your search argument with six or seven other major search engines. You can link to each of them from Yahoo (at the bottom of the search result page) to see what the results were from each of these search engines. An advantage of a Yahoo search is that if you locate an entry in Yahoo, it's likely to lead you to a Web site or an entire category of sites related to your search argument. Using search.com primarily searches the AltaVista index first but also lets you search the other major search engines as well. EasySearcher lets you choose from two indexes. One index provides access to six of the popular search engines. The second index provides access to specific keyword searchable databases on the Web.

Your Web browser also provides access to multiple search engines. If you click once on the "Search" button on the Internet Explorer toolbar, your browser displays a framed page that allows you to select AOL Netfind, Infoseek, Excite, and Lycos. Also provided is an "Other" button that provides access to HotBot, AltaVista, Web Crawler, Microsoft, Magellan, Yahoo, and NetGuide. If you select the button "Net Search" on the Netscape tool bar, your browser will access a page that has thirty-two different indexes categorized as search engines, Web guides, white and yellow pages, and topic indexes.

Each of the search engines or indexes provides numerous categories that can reduce your search time. Almost all have a business/finance section. You may have already noticed there is considerable overlap in the search engines provided at different access points. The overlap suggests that users with widely divergent interests consider these search engines the most useful.

Most if not all of the major search engines attempt to do something close to indexing the entire content of the World Wide Web. Once a site's pages have been indexed, the search engine will return periodically to the site to update the index. Some search engines give special weighting to words in the title, to in-subject descriptions and keywords listed in HTML META tags, to the first words on a page, and to the frequent recurrence (up to a limit) of a word on a page.

Because each search engine uses a somewhat different indexing and retrieval scheme, you may find yourself gravitating to one engine repeatedly. Most people find themselves favoring one search engine over another because the indexing and retrieval scheme seems consistent with how they categorize or index information. A good strategy is to search first at your favorite search engine and use the other available engines only when you fail to access information on your primary search engine. Remember that it may take a different perspective to uncover the information you are looking for.

How to Use a Search Engine

Searching for information becomes an individualistic exercise. Thus, search routines that your peers or superiors use may not be consistent with how you like to proceed. However, there are some general rules regarding searches. While generalization is difficult, here is an approach that can be adapted to your own style.

Begin your search using ideas and concepts (a selection provided as an alternative to keyword searches at most search engines) instead of just keywords. Always use more than one word in your search. Some search engines (Excite, for example) attempt to find relationships that exist between words and ideas, so the results of a search will contain words related to the concepts for which you are searching.

Most search engines present the results sorted by the relevance of the information on the page (this depends on the search engine's relevance rules). Thus, if you are searching for "accounting rules" the search engine's first result might be the page with the largest occurrence of the words *accounting* and *rules* on the same page. Besides the relevance ordering, most search engines provide additional means for narrowing your search. This takes the form of additional links related to your topic. Infoseek uses a related topics index, Excite uses links titled "More Like This Link," and Lycos also provides a section for additional information related to your topic.

Use descriptive, specific words as opposed to general ones. For example, a search for "current liabilities" will return much more specific results than a search for "liabilities." Of course "accounts payable" is even more specific. If you are interested in the accounts payable for a specific firm, you might search for "accounts payable" and "firmname." Some engines provide the ability to sort the search results by site. This presents several pages from the same site, thus reducing your information search when one site has multiple documents relevant to your search.

When searching for a phrase such as "management discussion" or "debt covenants," where you want the words in that order, enclose the phrase in quotes. A search on management discussion returns all pages with any or all of those words, in any order somewhere on the page. However, a search on "management discussion" just finds pages with that exact phrase on the page.

These general search hints should reduce the number of pages returned when searching for a topic you are interested in or have been assigned to research. However, you can expect to have more pages than you might be willing or have time to deal with. For example, searching the Excite search engine for the phrase "tax law" produces five thousand pages. How can you reduce the number of pages returned even more? One method of reducing the page count is to add terms to your search and search only the returned pages. Most search engines provide this option and if you have more specific terms available, we can reduce the number of pages drastically. For example, with Excite you have the option to power search, which guides you through restricting your search using several methods. Alternatively you can initially use special search operators, some of which we discuss below. This is not a complete list of operators and you should check the search tips section of your specific search engine.

Character Operators

These signs tell the search engine how to narrow your search. When these options are used, do not leave any space between the sign and the word. Not all search engines use these operators.

Plus (+): If you put a plus sign directly in front of a word, all the documents retrieved will contain that word. So if you search for +tax+law, you will retrieve pages with the words *tax* and *law*. On Excite, that returns more than 12,760 pages. Notice the difference it makes searching for the phrase "tax law" and the words *tax* and *law*. Because our objective is to reduce the number of pages returned, let us combine the phrase and plus sign to narrow our search for tax laws. Let us try "tax law" and *state*. The combination +"tax law"+state returns only 600 pages on the Excite search engine. Finally, the combination +"tax law"+state+Minnesota returns only 314 pages. Thus, we can progressively reduce the number of return pages as we become more specific with our search terms and tell the engine what must occur on the page and in what order.

Minus (-): If you put a minus sign directly in front of a word, the search engine will NOT retrieve documents containing that word. So if you search for "tax law"+state-federal, Excite will return only 524 pages instead of the 600 pages it returned when "tax law"+state was used.

Pipe (|): This character tells the Infoseek search engine that you want a search that moves from general to specific. Continuing with the tax law example, "tax law"|state produces 836 pages. Thus, the pipe allows you to specify a category and then search within that category for pages containing words specific to your search.

Wildcard ($ or *): These operators are used by Lycos ($) and Yahoo (*) to allow you to search for word variations. For example, Liab$ or Liab* will search for occurrences of the basic word *Liability*. If you are not sure how to spell a firm name, these same operators allow you to search based on the letters you do know. For example, assume you are not sure how to spell *Deloitte Touche* (big assumption but bear with me). You can search Lycos with the following: Deloi$ AND Touc$. The results provide a Web page produced by Deloitte and Touche in the first ten Web pages returned.

Boolean Operators

Boolean operators tell the search engine to allow you to search for documents that contain exactly the words for which you are looking. Boolean operators include AND, OR, AND NOT, and parentheses. These operators must appear in ALL CAPS and with a space on each side in order to work.

AND: Documents found must contain all words joined by the AND operator. For example, to find documents that contain the words *FASB*, *pensions*, and *costs*, enter: FASB AND pensions AND costs.

OR: Documents found must contain at least one of the words joined by OR. For example, to find documents that contain the phrase "balance sheet" or the word *asset*, enter: "Balance sheet" OR asset.

AND NOT: Documents found cannot contain the word that follows the term AND NOT. For example, to find documents that contain information about financial derivatives, you might enter: Derivative AND NOT calculus.

( ): Parentheses are used to group portions of Boolean queries together for more complicated queries. For example, to find documents with information about the risk of loss or losses associated with financial derivatives you might enter: "Financial Derivative" AND (risk OR loss).

Often the character operators can be used instead of the Boolean operator. The best search strategy involves using combinations of phrases using different operators to access Web pages containing the information you need. Some search engines allow character operators and Boolean operators to be used in the same search phrase, but others do not. If you are not sure, try a combination. The search engine will inform you whether the combination is possible. Your proficiency with search engines can greatly reduce the information acquisition time and thus the cost of any applied research project.

Evaluation of Information Sources

Information accessed on the Internet suffers, at times, from credibility. Because no oversight committee determines the content of Web pages, researchers using the Internet must develop criteria for evaluating the information sources available through this medium. Whatever criteria you develop, consider the following information about sources and search engines used.

Information Source Credibility

All information sources on the Web are not created equal. Consequently, you should develop a reliability index associated with the sources providing information. High on the list of reliable information sources should be government sites (U.S. Treasury), academic institutions (University of Chicago), respected private organizations (Tax Analysts), and some reputable commercial sites (Microsoft).

In addition, you should consider whether the information provided is available in other formats you can get. For example, congressional bills are available through other sources (i.e., printed documents). Thus, high reliability should be associated with the Internet site "Thomas," which is a government source with information also available in another medium.

Also consider whether the proper references to underlying sources on which the presented material relies upon are provided. In other words, if the information makes a factual (versus opinion) statement that relies on other documentation, can you obtain the other document source to verify the statement?

Search Engine Credibility

All search engines are not created equal. Some search engines just use a "robot" that scours the Internet to create a Web database. Except for the search routine imposed on the robot, no evaluation of the material collected is provided. On the other hand, some search engines collect information to be used to create "subject directories." These "directories" are built by members of the company's staff or by individuals hired on a contract basis to create the directory. This provides a filter system that at least associates related information with a specific directory. Thus, a directory is unlikely to contain offensive or frivolous information. Yahoo is an example of a subject directory search engine; Lycos is a Web database. A beginning strategy is to search for the same information on several engines to learn which one(s) is most useful to you.

Although you will ultimately decide which search engine and information source is credible and useful for your research project, criteria suggested here are similar to those used for research projects using other media. The rules that apply there apply equally when using the Internet.

Notes:

_____

_____

_____

_____

_____

_____

_____

_____

_____

_____

_____

_____

_____

_____

_____

_____

_____

Exercise 2-4   Name: _____
Using Search Engines   Section: _____

Instructions: Complete each of the following by accessing the information using Internet resources. Provide the address you used to access the information.

Explain the difference between searching using "Accounting AND Derivatives" and "Accounting OR Derivatives." Which search will produce the most pages?

_____

_____

_____

_____

Choose two search engines. Search for the following phrase on each search engine: "Health Care Costs." How many pages are returned on each search engine?

_____

_____

If there is a difference, can you give a reason for the difference?

_____

_____

If not, what can you add to this phrase to make it relate to accounting issues?

_____

_____

Does this reduce the number of pages returned? _____

Exercise 2-5   Name: _____
Locating Congressional Information   Section: _____

Instructions: Complete the following by accessing the information using Internet resources. Provide the address you used to access the information.

Congress is always talking about capital gains tax rates. Provide information about one House bill that has a capital gains provision (e.g., who sponsored, where it is, does it increase or decrease rates?).

_____

_____

_____

_____

_____

_____

_____

Exercise 2-6   **Name:** _____

Locating Accounting Information Sources   **Section:** _____

Instructions: Complete each of the following by accessing the information using Internet resources. Provide the address you used to access the information.

The Financial Accounting Standards Board (FASB) has been considering the issue of derivatives exposure. Can you obtain a copy of a comment letter concerning the FASB's proposed rules?

       YES   NO

Source address: _____

What company or entity wrote the letter? _____

If the letter were written by someone representing a company, try to locate the home page for that company and answer the following:

Name of company: _____

Location of company: _____

Type of business: _____

Number of employees: _____

Major products or services: _____

Source address: _____

Exercise 2-7   Name: _____
Locating Information Resources   Section: _____

Instructions: Complete the following by accessing the information using Internet resources. Provide the address you used to access the information.

Obtain a syllabus for an Accounting class that covers the same topics you expect to cover in this class.

Where did you obtain the syllabus? _____

What other information about courses, curriculum, and the college or university is available at that site?

_____

_____

_____

_____

_____

_____

ONLINE RESOURCES

Earlier in the chapter we indicated that this section would receive the least weight in terms of the information provided. However, the resources provided here should be less subject to change and more likely to update site and information changes publicly. The resources cover a variety of information and literally days could be spent searching each of these sites. While spending days searching these sites might not be an efficient use of your time, you should scan these sites to see what information they contain. The most incredible thing about these sites is they are available to you whenever you need them.

Government Resources

SEC (http://www.sec.gov): This site provides, in addition to many other information items, financial information about firms that file with the SEC. The financial statements are complete but must be searched by company name only.

GAO (http://www.gao.gov): The General Accounting Office supports this site and provides access to many reports by the GAO. Check out the GAO Reports and Testimony or Special Publications and Software.

GSA (http://www.info.gov/): This site is the government information exchange, sponsored by the General Services Administration. It provides access to nearly all government databases and information sources by topic. If you are not sure where government information might be found, look here first.

FedWorld (http://www.fedworld.gov/): The National Technical Information Service sponsors this site and it is the official resource for government-sponsored U.S. and worldwide scientific, technical, engineering, and business-related information. This is an excellent site to consider when you are not sure about where to find a federal document or file.

Thomas (http://thomas.loc.gov): The Legislature sponsors this site through the Library of Congress. It contains information about legislation for the most current session of Congress plus one prior session. Users can search for legislation by bill number, topic, title, or enactment.

Market Resources

New York Stock Exchange (http://www.nyse.com): The New York Stock Exchange (NYSE) Web site, designed for use by investors, students, and teachers, provides links to market databases, new company issues, links to some (but not all) companies traded on the exchange, and other market information.

American Stock Exchange (http://www.amex.com): The American Stock Exchange provides similar information to the NYSE. An interesting feature is the section on options and derivatives.

NASDAQ (http://nasdaq.com): The NASDAQ site provides, in addition to general market information, a list of the NASDAQ top 100 firms and a company index searchable by company name. Audio news broadcasts and interviews with corporate CEOs will likely be available when you read this.

Accounting Information Resources

AAA (http://www.rutgers.edu/Accounting/raw/aaa): The AAA (American Accounting Association) is an association of accounting academics and professionals concerned about accounting research and teaching. Links to information about specific accounting topics and areas are available here.

FASB (http://www.rutgers.edu/Accounting/raw/fasb/): The FASB (Financial Accounting Standards Board) site provides summaries and status of all FASB projects, as well as information about new exposure drafts and technical bulletins.

AICPA (http://www.aicpa.org/): The AICPA (American Institute of Certified Public Accountants) site has more than three thousand pages of information. Included in those pages are a hot topic section and a directory of information about assurance services, AICPA conferences, state societies, boards, and online AICPA publications.

IMA (http://www.rutgers.edu:80/Accounting/raw/ima/): The IMA site provides information on IMA Materials, links to Chapters and Councils, Member Interest Groups, and information about being or becoming a CMA (Certified Management Accountant).

RAW (http:/www.rutgers.edu/Accounting/raw/): The RAW (Rutgers Accounting Network) sponsors some of the sites listed here and is one of the largest accounting information sources in the world. It is a member of the international accounting network and is mirrored at several international sites. It is sponsored by the State University of New Jersey at Rutgers and supported by the National Center for Automated Information Research.

International Accounting Programs and Services

Nordic Accounting Network (http://www.nan.shh.fi/nan.html): The Department of Accounting sponsors this site at the Swedish School of Economics and Business Administration in Helsinki, Finland. Links to various European sites are provided.

The Summa Project (http://summa.cs.bham.ac.uk/): The Summa Project, based at the University of Birmingham in the United Kingdom, provides information for accounting academics and other professionals.

The Institute of Chartered Accountants in Ireland (http://www.icai.ie/): The ICAI provides information on accountancy in Ireland, the Chartered Accountants Tax Summary, information about ICAI Publications, and a guide for Overseas Students.

CONCLUSION

The objective of this chapter was to provide some technical competency, search strategies, and information resources to consider as you begin to develop your applied research skills. Remember that the Internet and the possibilities for using the Internet change daily. However, with a firm grasp of the material in this chapter, the cost of incorporating those changes into your research skill set will be small.

Exercise 2-8
An Introduction to SEC EDGAR

Name: _____

Section: _____

Instructions: For this project you need to access the SEC EDGAR databases using the Internet. Once you have linked to the EDGAR home page, you need to access the section titled "Form Definitions" and find the following information regarding the two forms assigned to you.

The forms assigned to you are based on the last two digits of your social security number.

Next to last digit	Form		Last digit	Form
0	8K		0	S20
1	10K		1	S8
2	10Q		2	S6
3	F1		3	S3
4	F2		4	S2
5	F3		5	S1
6	F4		6	N4
7	18K		7	N3
8	6K		8	N2
9	X-17A-5		9	N1A

For each form, prepare a brief (two or three lines) summary of the description of the form.

FORM: _____   _____

_____

_____

_____

FORM: _____   _____

_____

_____

_____

Exercise 2-9   Name: _____
Locating Information Resources   Section: _____

Instructions: Complete each of the following by accessing the information using Internet resources. Provide the address you used to access the information.

Your supervisor has indicated that he or she is concerned about whether the correct exchange rate was used to translate a new client's financial statements for an Italian subsidiary consolidated in the U.S. parent company's statements. Because another accounting firm handled the client the previous year, the manager has asked you to determine the exchange rate for Italian lire at the end of the most recent calendar year.

Source address: _____

Exchange rate–Italian lire for U.S. dollars: _____

You have a client in the state of Nebraska who is thinking about expanding her or his business into one of the following states–Iowa, South Dakota, Colorado, or Kansas. The client is concerned about the amount of property and corporate taxes he or she is likely to encounter in these states. Provide an analysis that shows how each of these states ranked nationally with regard to these types of taxes in the fourth quarter of the most recent calendar year. How do these states compare with Nebraska?

Source address: _____

_____

_____

_____

_____

_____

Exercise 2-10   **Name:** _____

Using SEC EDGAR   **Section:** _____

Instructions: For this project you need to access the SEC EDGAR databases using the Internet. Once you have linked to the EDGAR home page, you need to access the section titled "Tools and Utilities." Link to "CIK Code and Ticker Symbol Utilities" from within "Tools and Utilities."

Use "CIK Code and Ticker Symbol Utilities" to search for companies that have names that use your initials. In the input box titled <u>Input as much of the company as you know</u>, enter your initials and have the system search for corporations in which your initials are in the name. If there are no matches, then use your initials in a different order. If no matches are found using three initials, then use two of your initials and redo the search. After you have found some companies based on your initials, list the companies you will review. Then return to the EDGAR home page.

What are the names of at least three companies you found?

Company Name: _____

Company Name: _____

Company Name: _____

Explain the links between the company names above and your initials:

_____

_____

_____

At the EDGAR home page, go to "Search EDGAR Archives" and follow the instructions for searching for the filings of the companies you identified above. Enter the name of the company you are researching in the box. Note the forms filed, if any, for the company searched. Continue to search different companies until you find one that has filed a form 10-Q during the past year.

Company: _____

From the listing of filings made by this firm, complete the following:

Most recent form (any type) filed: _____

Date of filing: _____

Did the corporation file a 10-K for the most recent year? _____

If so, when? _____

What is the date of the most recent 10-Q filing? _____

Link to the most recent 10-Q filing and complete the following:

Date of most recent 10-Q filing: _____

What is the amount of total assets? _____

What is the amount of total revenues? _____

Did the company report income before extraordinary items? _____

If so, what is the amount? _____

Exercise 2-11   **Name:** _____
Locating Information Resources   **Section:** _____

Instructions: Complete each of the following by accessing the information using Internet resources. Provide the address you used to access the information.

Provide a summary of the latest FASB proposed statement on the reporting for derivatives and similar financial instruments.

Source address: _____

_____

_____

_____

_____

The AICPA issued a report concerning the future of the accounting profession. Obtain information about the types of services that the AICPA sees as viable for the future accountant in the information age. Indicate what three of those services are and provide a short summary.

Source address: _____

_____

_____

_____

_____

Exercise 2-12   Name: _____
Locating Information Resources   Section: _____

Instructions: Complete each of the following by accessing the information using Internet resources. Provide the address you used to access the information.

The United States has exchanged instruments of ratification for new income tax treaties with several countries. It also terminated several outstanding treaties. Using only information provided by the IRS determine which countries and treaties had provisions that became effective in 1997 and which countries for which treaties were terminated on January 1997.

Source address: _____

_____

_____

_____

_____

_____

Using the Internet, obtain a spreadsheet containing the consolidated balance sheet information for PepsiCo for years ending December 30, 1995, and December 31, 1994.

Source address: _____

How many shares did PepsiCo add to treasury stock between 1994 and 1995?

_____

Chapter 3
Applied Research in
Financial Accounting and Reporting

INTRODUCTION

The distinction between domains such as financial accounting and taxation is based not so much upon the type of problems or issues encountered but upon the sources of authoritative guidance. For instance, guidance in the financial accounting area focuses on generally accepted accounting principles (GAAP) while guidance for taxation issues focuses on statutory, administrative, and judicial sources. In both financial accounting and taxation, similar issues ("what," "when," or "how" questions) and contexts (compliance or planning) may be encountered. The difference lies in the sources of professional guidance.

AUTHORITATIVE SOURCES OF GENERALLY ACCEPTED ACCOUNTING PRINCIPLES

For financial accounting and reporting, whether a certified public accountant must audit the financial statements defines the domain. To receive a "clean" opinion by the auditor, the financial statements must be prepared in conformance with generally accepted accounting principles.

The Code of Professional Conduct for members of the American Institute of Certified Public Accountants (AICPA) requires members to prepare financial statements in conformance with GAAP. An AICPA member is prohibited from expressing an opinion that financial statements are in conformance with GAAP if there is a material departure from GAAP (unless the use of GAAP would produce misleading financial statements).

The AICPA defines generally accepted accounting principles as Financial Accounting Standards Board (FASB) Standards and Interpretations, Accounting Principles Board (APB) Opinions, and American Institute of Certified Public Accountants (AICPA) Accounting Research Bulletins. For transactions or circumstances not covered in these pronouncements, other sources of authoritative literature may be used. Frequently, this literature consists of documents considered to possess substantial authoritative support. This support comes from an authoritative body having considered the issue via a promulgation process, including due process, and voted for issuance of the document.

For financial accounting and reporting, there are multiple authoritative organizations. These include the Financial Accounting Standards Board (FASB) and its predecessors (APB and CAP), as well as the Emerging Issues Task Force (EITF), the Governmental Accounting Standards

Board (GASB), and the Accounting Standards Division of the American Institute of Certified Public Accountants.

The Financial Accounting Standards Board promulgates financial accounting and reporting standards for all public and nonpublic enterprises except state and local governments. The FASB issues various types of pronouncements with different levels of authority. The FASB issues Statements of Financial Accounting Standards (SFAS), Statements of Financial Accounting Concepts (SFAC), Interpretations, Technical Bulletins, and Special Reports (Guides to Implementation). Statements of Financial Accounting Standards establish new standards or modify previous standards issued by the FASB or a predecessor. Statements of Financial Accounting Concepts provide the theoretical underpinnings on which they base the financial accounting and reporting standards. Technical Bulletins clarify and explain underlying standards or areas not covered in existing standards. Special Reports or Guides to Implementation address implementation issues for standards.

The AICPA recognizes the FASB as the body that establishes financial accounting and reporting standards for nongovernmental entities. The Securities and Exchange Commission considers FASB statements and interpretations to have "substantial authoritative support." For additional information regarding the Financial Accounting Standards Board and its mission, link via the Internet to the FASB's home page at http://www.rutgers.edu/Accounting/raw/fasb/. In particular, read "Facts about FASB."

The two predecessors of the FASB, appointed by the AICPA, were the Committee on Accounting Procedure (CAP) and the Accounting Principles Board (APB). The Committee on Accounting Procedure issued Accounting Research Bulletins while the Accounting Principles Board issued Opinions. While each group suffered from concerns regarding a lack of independence and a lack of due process, many of their pronouncements still constitute GAAP.

The FASB established the Emerging Issues Task Force (EITF) to provide quick and timely guidance on implementation concerns and novel or emerging issues. EITF consensus positions are considered part of the hierarchy of GAAP.

The Governmental Accounting Standards Board (GASB) provides financial accounting and reporting guidance for state and local governmental units. Similar to the FASB, the GASB issues Statements, Interpretations, Concept Statements, and Technical Bulletins.

Within the American Institute of Certified Public Accountants (AICPA), the Accounting Standards Executive Committee (AcSEC) represents the Accounting Standards Division in matters regarding financial accounting and reporting issues. AcSEC issues Statements of Position (SOP), which are considered another part of the hierarchy of GAAP. In addition, the Accounting Standards Division also issues Practice Bulletins. For additional information regarding the AICPA, use the Internet to link to the AICPA's home page at http://www.aicpa.org/.

The financial accounting and reporting requirements for entities required to report to the Securities and Exchange Commission (SEC) are set by the SEC. The SEC, an independent agency of the federal government, possesses the statutory authority to prescribe all of its required filings and this includes form, content, and accounting methods. The SEC issues Financial Reporting Releases (FRRs) and Accounting and Auditing Enforcement Releases (AAERs). The SEC's positions on accounting and auditing issues are contained in the FRRs. The AAERs communicate enforcement actions regarding violations of securities laws. Additional guidance regarding disclosure requirements is provided in the SEC's Staff Accounting Bulletins (SABs). Additional information regarding the SEC can be on the Internet at the address http://www.sec.gov.

As international accounting and auditing issues become more prevalent, the International Accounting Standards Committee (IASC) will likely play a more significant role in shaping GAAP. While the IASC's pronouncements, Statements of International Accounting Standards (SIAS), do not currently constitute GAAP, these pronouncements will influence GAAP in the United States and could be adopted as GAAP by the FASB.

HIERARCHY OF GENERALLY ACCEPTED ACCOUNTING PRINCIPLES

As previously discussed, many different pronouncements are considered to constitute GAAP and their level of authority varies. For example, the highest level of authority, deemed Category (A), consists of the FASB Statements and Interpretations, the APB Opinions, and the AICPA Accounting Research Bulletins. Lower levels of authority are denoted Categories B, C, and D. It is important that you understand this hierarchy. When conducting applied research, you must distinguish between solutions with a low level of authoritative support and those with a higher level of authoritative support.

	Pronouncement	Issuing Body
Category A	Statements of Financial Accounting Standards (SFAS)	Financial Accounting Standards Board (FASB)
	FASB Interpretations (FIN)	FASB
	Accounting Principles Board Opinions (APB)	Accounting Principles Board (APB)
	Accounting Research Bulletins (ARB)	AICPA Committee on Accounting Procedures (CAP)
Category B	FASB Technical Bulletins (FTB)	FASB
	AICPA Industry Audit and Accounting Guides	AICPA Committees or Task Forces
	AICPA Statements of Position (SOP)	AICPA Accounting Standards Executive Committee (AcSEC)
Category C	Consensus Positions of FASB's Emerging Issues Task Force (EITF)	FASB's Emerging Issues Task Force (EITF)
	AICPA (AcSEC) Practice Bulletins	AICPA (AcSEC)
Category D	AICPA Accounting Interpretations (AIN)	AICPA staff
	FASB Implementation Guides (Q's and A's)	FASB staff
	Industry Practices	

As depicted above, Category A pronouncements represent the highest level of authority while Category D materials represent the lowest level of authority.

The AICPA has explicitly defined the hierarchy of GAAP for both nongovernmental and governmental entities in SOP 93-3. Following is a table depicting the hierarchy of the two types of entities.

Non governmental Entities	Category	Governmental Entities

SFASs
FINs
APBs
ARBs
	A	GASB Statements
		GASB Interpretations
		AICPA and FASB Pronouncements
		   Made Applicable by GASB
		   Statements or Interpretations

FTBs AICPA Industry Audit Guides SOPs	B	GASB Technical Bulletins Applicable AICPA Audit Guides, Accounting Guides, and SOPs
EITFs AcSEC Practice Bulletins	C	GASB EITFs Applicable AcSEC Practice Bulletins
AINs Q's and A's	D	GASB Q's and A's

SFACs
AICPA Issues Papers
SIASs
GASB Statements, Interpretations, and
   Technical Bulletins
Pronouncements of Other Professional
   Associations or Regulatory
   Agencies
Accounting Textbooks, Handbooks, or
   Articles
	E	GASB Concept Statements
		Non-applicable Pronouncements of the
		   AICPA, FASB, or GASB
		SFACs
		SIASs
		Pronouncements of Other Professional
		   Associations or Regulatory Agencies
		AICPA Technical Practice Aids
		Accounting Textbooks, Handbooks, or
		   Articles

Note that pronouncements that do not specifically address an issue may help in resolving an issue through analogous reasoning. In such instances, it is important for the researcher to determine the similarities that exist and those that differentiate the issue upon which the pronouncement is based and the problem or issue on which the research is being conducted.

Become familiar with the tables above and keep them handy for future use.

APPLIED RESEARCH IN ATTESTATION, AUDITING, AND OTHER PROFESSIONAL SERVICES

Accountants involved in providing attestation and assurance services conduct applied professional research related to determining the propriety of certain auditing and attestation practices as well as standards of conduct as a professional. The source of authoritative guidance is the American Institute of Certified Public Accountants (AICPA). The AICPA also provides guidance regarding other professional services such as accounting and review services or prospective financial information services.

The Auditing Standards Board (ASB) of the AICPA focuses its attention on auditing matters. It promulgates Statements on Auditing Standards (SASs) and other authoritative guidance. The Auditing Standards Division issues Interpretations, Auditing Research Monographs, Auditing Procedure Studies, and Audit Risk Alerts.

Although the applications in this text focus primarily on financial accounting and reporting issues as well as applications in taxation, the primary research process and tools are applicable to issues surrounding attestation, auditing, or other professional services. As explained in Chapter 1, the primary difference is the source of the applicable authoritative literature.

Exercise 3-1 Name: _____

FASB Section: _____

Instructions: Using an Internet browser, search for information to answer the following questions. Be sure to provide the address where the information was found.

Locate the home page for the FASB on the Internet.

Source address: _____

What is the mission of the FASB and why are accounting standards essential?

_____

_____

_____

_____

Define or describe each of the following:

FASB: _____

_____

Financial Accounting Foundation: _____

_____

Financial Accounting Standards Advisory Council: _____

_____

_____

Briefly describe how topics are added to the FASB's technical agenda:

_____

_____

_____

The FASB uses what four criteria in determining to add a topic to its agenda?

_____

_____

_____

_____

Who are the current FASB board members?

_____   _____

_____   _____

_____   _____

_____   _____

Who is the current chairperson of the Emerging Issues Task Force?

_____

Exercise 3-2 Name: _____

The FARS System Section: _____

Instructions: Using an Internet browser, search for information to answer the following questions. Be sure to provide the address where the information was found.

What is FARS? _____

_____

Source address: _____

What are the names of the five infobases contained in FARS?

_____ _____

_____ _____

_____

What is the name of the search and retrieval software (interface) used for FARS?

_____

Can you find the home page of the company that produces this search and retrieval software?

_____

Source address:_____

Company name:_____

Exercise 3-3   Name: _____

The AICPA   Section: _____

Instructions: Using an Internet browser, search for information to answer the following questions. Be sure to provide the address where the information was found.

Link to the AICPA home page and answer the following questions.

Under what heading can you find information about the AICPA and its mission?

_____

Source address: _____

What are some important dates in the history of the AICPA?

Date: Importance:

_____   _____

_____   _____

_____   _____

What is the most recent number of members in the AICPA? _____

Under what heading can you obtain information about the Uniform CPA Examination?

_____

What are the five major components of the AICPA Mission Statement?

_____   _____

_____   _____

_____

Exercise 3-4   Name: _____
The SEC   Section: _____

Instructions: Using an Internet browser, search for information to answer the following questions. Be sure to provide the address where the information was found.

Briefly describe the SEC: _____

_____

_____

_____

_____

Source address: _____

Briefly describe the Securities Act of 1933:_____

_____

_____

_____

_____

Briefly describe the Securities Act of 1934:_____

_____

_____

_____

_____

What are the two basic objectives of the "truth in securities" law?

_____

_____

_____

_____

What division of the SEC is responsible for firms meeting certain disclosure requirements?

_____

Chapter 4
Accessing Professional
Literature Databases

INTRODUCTION

Applied professional research requires identifying a problem or issue and locating the appropriate authority to solve that issue. Historically, research was accomplished using printed material published by the Financial Accounting Standards Board and the American Institute of Certified Public Accountants. The Accounting Standards, Current Text, and AICPA Professional Standards comprised approximately five volumes of printed material. Within the past several years, the authoritative literature has been adapted so that computer searches are possible. However, distinct differences exist in research strategies using hard-copy sources and electronic media.

Hard Copy vs. Electronic Media

The Financial Accounting Standards Board publishes the *Original Pronouncements of the Accounting Standards* in a printed two-volume set. If you wanted to research the topic *depreciation*, you would turn to the topical index at the back of the *Original Pronouncements*. Exhibit 4-1 is an example of the results you would find (June 1, 1996):

	Original Pronouncements	Current Text	EITF and Other
DEPRECIATION			
See Disclosure			
Accelerated			
..Temporary Differences,			
Regulated Operations..............	FAS 109, ¶288	Re6.128	
Accounting Changes..................	APB20, ¶23-24	A06.119-120	
Accounting Policy Disclosure....	APB22, ¶14	A10.106	
Applicability to Not-for-Profit			
Organizations...........................	FAS93, ¶5-6	D40.101-101B	
....	FAS93, ¶35-36		
Appraisals Not Allowed	APB6, ¶17	D40.102	
Basic Principle	APB6, ¶17	D40.101-102	
....	ARB43, Ch.9C, ¶5	D40.104	
....	FAS93, ¶5-6		
....	FAS93, ¶35-37		
....	FAS109, ¶288		
Deferred Tax Accounting			
Revaluation of Assets for Tax			
Purposes			EITF 84-43
Definition	ARB43, Ch.9C, ¶5	D40.401	

EXHIBIT 4-1

Notice that this is a topical search using an index. A person or persons compiled this index by generating an alphabetical list of accounting topics. The person then identified the standards that addressed each topic and created a list of subheadings. Notice that the subheadings are also in alphabetical order; that is, *accelerated depreciation* comes before *accounting changes*. The same topical list was use to develop cross-references for the Current Text and for the EITF Questions and Answers.

The most important factor in performing hard-copy searches is that the information is grouped by topic alphabetically. A researcher would need to find each standard in the text. The standard might be read in its entirety to find appropriate paragraphs. The researcher may also photocopy the relevant material.

The hard-copy version of the standards is divided into subunits or paragraphs for ease in referencing the material. Exhibit 4-2 illustrates a portion of a page from the hard-copy version of ARB 43, Chapter 4.

ARB 43   Accounting Research Bulletin

finished goods, is difficult because of the variety of problems encountered in the allocation of costs and charges. For example, under some circumstances, items such as idle facility expense, excessive spoilage, double freight, and rehandling costs may be so abnormal as to require treatment as current period charges rather than as a portion of the invent-ory cost. Also, general and administrative expenses should be included as period charges, except for the portion of such expenses that may be clearly related to production and thus constitute a part of inventory costs (product charges). Selling expenses constitute no part of inventory costs.   It should also be recognized that the exclusion of all overheads from inventory costs does not constitute an accepted accounting procedure. The exercise of judgment in an individual situation involves a consideration of the adequacy of the procedures of the cost accounting system in use, the soundness of the principles thereof, and their consistent application.

Statement 4

Cost for inventory purposes may be determined under any one of several assumptions as to the flow of cost factors (such as first-in first-out, average, and last-in first-out); the major objective in selecting a method should be to choose the one which, under the circumstances, most clearly reflects periodic income.

Discussion

6. The cost to be matched against revenue from a sale may not be the identified cost of the specific item which is sold, especially in cases in which

practical and appropriate. The business operations in some cases may be such as to make it desirable to apply one of the acceptable methods of determining cost to one portion of the inventory or components thereof and another of the acceptable methods to other portions of the inventory.

7. Although selection of the method should be made on the basis of the individual circumstances, it is obvious that financial statements will be more useful if uniform methods of inventory pricing are adopted by all companies within a given industry.

Statement 5

A departure from the cost basis of pricing the inventory is required when the utility of the goods is no longer as great as its cost. Where there is evidence that the utility of goods, in their disposal in the ordinary course of business, will be less than cost, whether due to physical deterioration, obsolescence, changes in price levels, or other causes, the difference should be recognized as a loss of the current period.   This is generally accomplished by stating such goods at a lower level commonly designated as market.

Discussion

8. Although the cost basis ordinarily achieves the objective of a proper matching of costs and revenues, under certain circumstances cost may not be the amount properly chargeable against the revenues of future periods. A departure from cost is required in these circumstances because cost issatisfactory only if the utility of the goods has not

EXHIBIT 4-2

Researching with hard-copy sources poses several limitations. The first limitation is that your search is dependent upon the individual who indexed the material. The second limitation is that reading the index, finding and reading the referenced standards, and photocopying the appropriate material is time consuming. The third limitation is that because the material is indexed by topic, the search may not be exhaustive.

Electronic media searches are now available to make research more efficient and effective. Both the AICPA Professional Standards and the FASB Accounting Standards are available in electronic media. These programs allow you to search quickly and more thoroughly for information, retrieve that information, download it, and print it for later use. Once you understand the basic vocabulary, organization, and commands of an information database, you can easily transfer your knowledge and skills to almost any information base.

UNDERSTANDING INFOBASES

As a business student, you may have encountered databases. A database stores information in a structured format by defining cells, fields, and records. For example, a company may store its customer list in a database and define the fields as name, street address, city, state, zip code, and phone number. Employees could search the database, sort, and/or print using any of the named fields.

Electronically storing information in an organized way allows us to retrieve that information quickly. Imposing structure on information such as the customer list database is fairly simple. However, creating a database, or **infobase**, which deals with large chunks of information in paragraph form is much more complex. We refer to this type of database as an "infobase" because it contains large chunks of information instead of raw data.

An infobase is a collection of information organized so that it is searchable with software. It is indexed or categorized by words, numbers, and groups. The information contained in the infobase is divided into blocks or chunks of information. These blocks can be headings, sentences, paragraphs, pages, tables, or any other unit that is large enough to express a thought. In the professional literature databases for the AICPA Professional Standards and the Financial Accounting Standards Board FARS (Financial Accounting Research System), the blocks are most commonly titles, headings, and paragraphs. In infobase terminology, we refer to each of these individual blocks of information as a **record**.

The infobase divides the professional pronouncements into discreet pieces called records. These records may be a title or heading, a table of contents item, a paragraph, a memo, or a page of material. When you search the infobase, the software retrieves all records that contain your word or string of search terms, referred to as keywords. Keep in mind, the infobase does not search by subject or concept; it searches for exact matches to character strings that you have typed. Therefore, it is extremely important that you develop a strong accounting vocabulary because you must use the correct keywords to find the appropriate literature.

Financial Accounting Research System (FARS)

When you access the FARS infobase, the first item to appear is the title page. This page identifies the search system. While the accounting principles are issued by the Financial Accounting Standards Board, the Financial Accounting Research System (FARS) uses Folio Bound VIEWS search and retrieval software. We show the title page to FARS in Exhibit 4-3.

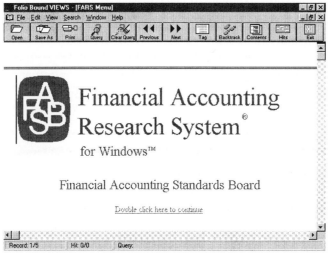

EXHIBIT 4-3

Follow the instructions on the screen and double click on the colored underlined text to use the FARS program. When you enter FARS, you will see the following main menu on your screen:

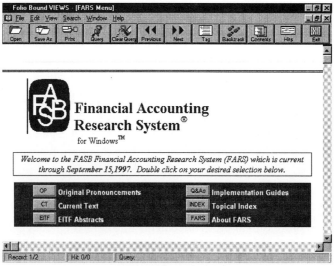

EXHIBIT 4-4

The main menu lists six items: four separate infobases, a topical index, and a brief overview of FARS. Following is a brief description of the contents of each item on the main menu.

Original Pronouncements

> This portion of the infobase contains the AICPA and FASB pronouncements. It is the two-volume hard copy version converted into database form. Volume I of the hardcopy version includes FASB Statements of Standards; Volume II contains the AICPA Pronouncements, the FASB Interpretations, the FASB Concept Statements, FASB Technical Bulletins, Topical Indexes, and Appendices. The electronic version of the pronouncements organizes the two volumes in a different order than the hard copy volumes. All of the pronouncements are in chronological order. Similar to the hard copy version, the pronouncements are included in their entirety with superseded and amended portions denoted. The table of contents for the Original Pronouncement section is shown in Exhibit 4-5. The citation abbreviations are shown in parentheses.

Current Text

> The Current Text infobase contains the same items found in the Volumes I and II of the hard-copy version. As you recall, the hard-copy version Volume I of the Current Text is a compilation of accounting treatment for the general standards. The compilation is by topic and listed in alphabetical order. The hard-copy version of Volume II of the current text includes industry standards. The current text cites the original pronouncements for authority on each topic.

EITF Abstracts

> The EITF Abstracts contain the full text of the EITF Abstracts, a list of task force members, general and administrative matters, other technical matters, a topical index, and a topical table of contents.

Implementation Guides Q & A

> The Implementation Guides Q & A contains implementation question and answers for certain FAS statements.

Topical Index

> The topical index is the same topical index that is found in the hard-copy version. It is in alphabetical order by subject.

About FARS

> This is a brief introduction of approximately two printed pages that outlines the contents of the other five menu items. It highlights the features of FARS and briefly explains the various ways to access information using the infobase.

The Original Pronouncements are the primary source of authority for applied professional research in accounting. Double click on the Original Pronouncements icon to see the table of contents as shown in Exhibit 4-5.

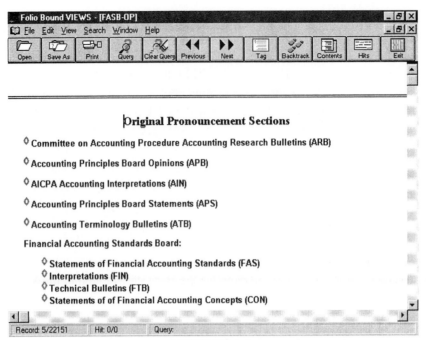

EXHIBIT 4-5

Notice that it lists all of the standards beginning with the Committee on Accounting Procedures to the present. The Original Pronouncements infobase is organized in chronological order by the date the standards were issued. You should become familiar with the abbreviations shown in parentheses to the right of each table of contents item. These abbreviations will be used to cite the authoritative literature when conducting research.

WORKING WITH THE INFOBASE

Windows, Views, and Links

The infobase is a collection of electronically stored information broken into blocks or chunks of information called records. When you are working in an infobase, you are in a **window**. A window is a framed area on your computer screen.

A **view** is a portion of the infobase that you have accessed. A **full view** contains all the records of the infobase. A **narrowed view** contains only part of the infobase. Views are accessed by entering the infobase in one of three ways–by the table of contents window, by the topical index, and by search queries.   Search queries are the most powerful means of searching; therefore, this text will concentrate on developing your skills for search queries.

The infobase uses links to access various portions of the infobase. The two most important links for research purposes are "jump links" and "pop-up links." Jump links are used as launch points to take you to a specific place in the database. Jump links can be icons, buttons, a magnifying glass, or a diamond. Clicking on these jump links will move you to a different part of the infobase. FARS also contains pop-up links which are indicated by red or colored footnotes embedded in the text. Clicking on these footnotes or pop-up links will open a small window containing additional information. Notice the diamond-shaped jump links to the left of each Original Pronouncement section in Exhibit 4-5.

The Toolbelt. The toolbelt allows you to use commands and access drop-down menus with one click of the left button on the mouse. The toolbelt allows you to open, save, and print files, search for information, and navigate through the infobase. We will discuss each button on the toolbelt in greater detail later in the text.

Navigating the Infobase

Moving around in the infobase is simple. You can move one line at a time, one hit at a time, or one view at a time. In addition, you can move forward, move backward, exit from views, toggle between multiple views, and perform additional searches. Mastering the toolbelt and keystroke commands is essential for efficiently using the infobase.

For now, we will look at some simple commands: the double click, the single click, the cursor arrows (right, left, up, down), page-up, and page-down. The double click with the mouse is used to activate a link to another portion of the database. When we position the cursor on a link, the cursor arrow changes to a hand. The single click with the left mouse button is used to activate the toolbelt and menu commands at the top of the screen. The cursor arrows move one space left or right, and one line up or down. The page-up and page-down keys move you one window forward or backward within the current view.

Getting Started with the Infobase. Recall that underlined words in colors are "link launch points," which you should double click to activate. First, enter the FARS system and double click at the link launch point to access the FARS menu. This menu will contain the six icons for the Original Pronouncements, Current Text, EITF Abstracts, Implementation Guides Q&A, Topical Index, and About FARS. Each of these icons represents a separate file of material. Double click on the icon (jump link) Original Pronouncements to access the Original Pronouncements. You will see the window as shown in Exhibit 4-6.

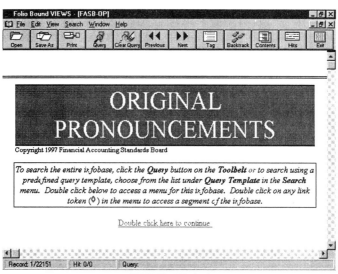

EXHIBIT 4-6

Let us examine the window. The toolbelt is at the top. The top line with commands (File, Edit, View, Search, Window, Help) are pull-down menus. You can pull these menus down by clicking on them once with the left mouse button. The commands in the boxes are toolbelt commands (Open, Save As, Print, Query, Clear Query, Previous, Next, Tag, Backtrack, Contents, Hits, and Exit). Although the toolbelt can be customized, we recommend that you do not alter the toolbelt since this text is based on default settings.

At the bottom left-hand corner of the window, you see the following:

Record: 1/22151

This means that you are in the first record of 22,151 records that are contained in the Original Pronouncements section of the infobase. To the right of this number, you see the term Hit: 0/0. This means that you have not accessed any portion of the infobase at this point. Notice that the query line is also blank. You can begin a query at this window or you can double click on the launch point to go to the next menu.

If you double click on the launch point, you will see the menu as shown in Exhibit 4-7.

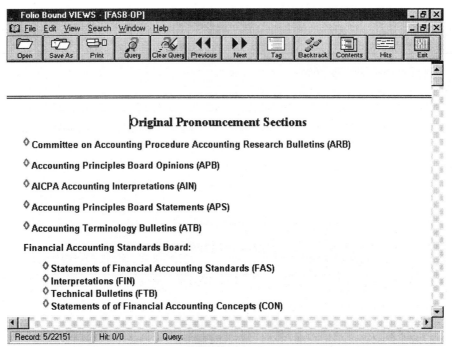

EXHIBIT 4-7

This is the table of contents for the Original Pronouncements. If you are extremely familiar with the accounting standards and know all the standards by number, you might use the jump link (red diamond) and move to the desired portion of the infobase. However, if you are conducting research, you would want to use the search or query command.

Searching the Infobase

To begin a search, click once on the "Query" box on the toolbelt. The following screen as shown in Exhibit 4-8 will appear:

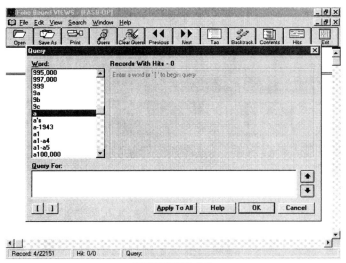

EXHIBIT 4-8

The Query command will activate several windows on your screen–a word window, a results window, and a query window. The word window is on the top left-hand side; it includes all words in the infobase. We will discuss the importance of the word window later. The results window is on the top right. After a query is typed in, the query and number of hits are shown in the results window. The Query For: window is at the bottom center of the screen. To perform a search, the search term is typed into the "Query For:" window, and then you press return (enter). The search term and the number of hits are shown in the results window on the top right. To look at the text of the results, simply press return (enter) again. The Query For window will disappear and the full text of your results will appear.

Let us search for the term depreciation. Exhibit 4-9 shows our results window:

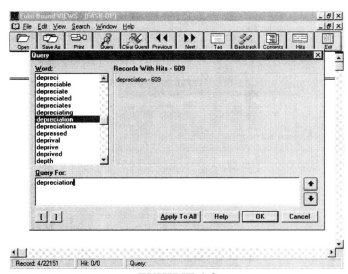

EXHIBIT 4-9

The Original Pronouncements infobase has 609 records that contain the term *depreciation*.

We must make an important distinction between hard-copy searches and infobase searches here. Recall that in a hard-copy search, we looked at the topical index for *depreciation*. The topical index provided the cross-references to the accounting standards that contained information on the subject of depreciation. There was no distinction between various forms of the word.

The infobase, however, is NOT a topical search. It is a character string search performed by a computer. Therefore, the computer looks for an exact match. Notice the word box. The word box shows that there are several variations of the word *depreciation*, which include *depreciable* (adjective), *depreciate* (verb), *depreciated* (past tense verb), *depreciates* (verb), *depreciating* (gerund), and *depreciations* (plural). Therefore, if you wanted to find all records that referred to the subject of depreciation, you would need to search all forms or variations of the word *depreciation*. In the next section, we will discuss shortcut methods to expand the search to include the derivations of a word.

After looking at the results window, press return (enter). This should activate the full text of your results, which is a narrowed view of the infobase. Exhibit 4-10 reveals the first page of the results for this search:

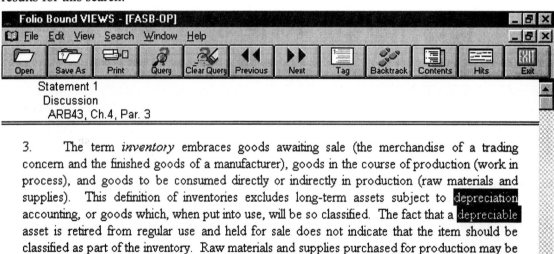

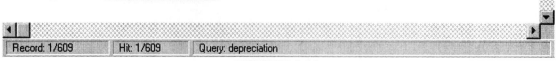

EXHIBIT 4-10

Notice the box between the toolbelt and the actual text. This area is called the "Reference Window" and identifies the citation of each hit from the infobase. Our results indicate that hit #1 is from Accounting Research Bulletin No. 43, Chapter 4, Paragraph 3. As you move through each hit in your results, this reference window will change. Although this reference window can be deleted or modified to show one or more lines, we recommend that novice users use the default setting of three lines.

Notice the numbers at the bottom of the screen: Record: 1/609 and Hit: 1/609. These two windows show where you are within the infobase or within the particular results of a query. Watching these numbers is important as you scroll through the narrowed view to track which records you have read. Notice that in some records, the word appears more than once.

Notice that the query term is highlighted throughout the results. The infobase search engine retrieved only those records where the word depreciation was found. A record can be a paragraph or more of text, a heading, or a table of contents item.

To move through the text of your results, you can click on the "Next" button on the toolbelt, or you can press "F3". Advance through the narrowed view using the Next or F3 command, and watch how the reference window at the top and record number at the bottom change as you move through the results. Notice that as you press Next or F3, you move to the next highlighted word and not necessarily to the next record.

Move through the document until you come to the following citation:
>   ARB 43: Restatement and Revision of Accounting Research Bulletins
>   Chapter 9: Depreciation
>   Section B — Depreciation on Appreciation

In the May 1997 version of the infobase, this was record 12/609, and the screen is shown in Exhibit 4-11.

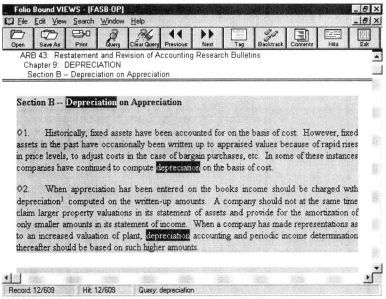

EXHIBIT 4-11

Notice that record 12 is not a paragraph, but a heading. Also, notice the diamond-shaped jump link in front of the record 13. This jump link indicates that additional information is contained therein. Double click on the jump link to access this information. Notice that in record 14, a colored (red) footnote appears at the end of the first sentence. This is a pop-up link. Clicking on the footnote or pop-up link will activate a small pop-up window with additional information or definitions. These pop-up links are similar to footnotes contained in the hard-copy of the text.

Superseded and Amended Material

Two other issues are important in using the infobase. Gray shading shows superseded material. Exhibit 4-11 reveals that records 12, 13, and 14 are superseded material.   Superseded material is included in the standards to familiarize accountants with the history of accounting treatment for a specific item. Occasionally, only portions of a standard are superseded.

A thick black bar in the left-hand margin denotes amended material. Exhibit 4-12 is an example of amended material that is taken from record 453/609 in our query for *depreciation*.

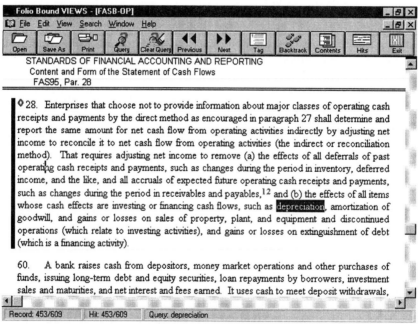

EXHIBIT 4-12

Capitalization and Spacing

The infobase ignores capitalization. Therefore, if you search for the term Depreciation or depreciation in either lower or mixed case, the results should be identical. However, because the infobase is programmed to match character strings, spacing is very important. For example, if you search the infobase for "FAS 87," there are 15 hits. If you search the infobase for "FAS87" with no space, you will find 485 hits.

Citing Material from the Infobase

When you refer to the literature in research reports, citing the EXACT location is important so that your supervisor, manager, or partner can trace and evaluate your research efforts. The appropriate cite can be found in the third line of the reference window. The cite should contain the statement number, chapter (if applicable), and paragraph number. For example, a complete cite would be ARB 43, Ch. 9, Par. 23.

Help. Help is accessible through a pull-down menu at the top or by pressing the F1 key. The help command contains an online tutorial for the infobase, as well as a query command for accessing help on a specific topic.

Exiting the Program. To exit the help menu or any portion of the program, simply click on the "X" in the top right-hand corner of your screen. The backtrack command on the toolbelt will back you up one step to the previous screen. You can use the backtrack command to back up to the FARS title page. To close the program you can either use the X key in the top right-hand corner of your screen or use the File pull down menu and exit the program.

Notes:

_____

_____

_____

_____

_____

_____

_____

_____

_____

_____

_____

_____

_____

_____

_____

_____

_____

_____

Exercise 4-1   Name: _____

Getting Acquainted with the Infobase   Section: _____

1.   There are four infobases in the FARS system. Read "About FARS." Explain the difference between the Original Pronouncements and the Current Text.

_____

_____

_____

_____

2.   Access the Current Text. How many total records are in the Current Text?

_____

3.   Access the Current Text section's table of contents. Double click on the jump link for "General Standards." How many records are contained in this portion of the infobase?

_____

4.   Click "Backtrack" on the toolbelt. Double click on "Industry Standards." How many records are in this portion of the Current Text infobase?

_____

5.   Click Backtrack on the toolbelt several times until you reach the main menu for the FARS system. Open the Original Pronouncements by double clicking on the icon. How many records are located in the Original Pronouncements?

_____

6.   Why are the number of records in the Current Text different from the number of records in the Original Pronouncements?

_____

_____

_____

_____

7.   Backtrack to the main menu of FARS. Double click on the EITF Abstracts to find the
         EITF Abstracts Menu. Double click on the jump link to read the Introduction. Answer
         the following questions:

         a)   When was the EITF formed? _____

         b)   What is the purpose of the EITF?

_____

_____

_____

_____

_____

_____

Exercise 4-2   **Name:** _____

Understanding the Contents of the Infobases Section: _____

1.   Open the Current Text. Using the Query button on the toolbelt, query the term
      consolidation—how many hits do you find?

      _____

2.   Look at the third line of the reference window. List the first cite found in the Current
      Text for the query *consolidation*.

      _____

3.   In what order do the Current Text cites appear?

      _____

      _____

4.   Scroll down through the text of the results on your search in the Current Text. Do you
      see any superseded material (shaded text) in your results? If so, identify one superseded
      paragraph.

      _____

5.   Page down to the record that contains the cite A10.106 in the Current Text. Notice the
      cross-referencing at the end of the paragraph in brackets. What is the reference number?

      _____

6.   Copy the paragraph from A10.106. How many lines of text are shown on the screen? Is
      there any superseded material in this paragraph?

      _____

      _____

      _____

      _____

      _____

7.   Open the Original Pronouncements. Search for the term *consolidation*—how many cites do you find?

        _____

8.   What is the first cite you found in the Original Pronouncements?

        _____

9.   In what order are your results found in the Original Pronouncements?

        _____

        _____

10.   Scroll down through the text of the results on your search for *consolidation* in the Original Pronouncements. Do you see any superseded material? If so, cite one superseded paragraph.

        _____

        _____

11.   Page down to the record that contains the cite APB 22, Par. 13. How many lines of text are shown on the screen? Is there any superseded material in this paragraph?

        _____

        _____

        _____

12.   Compare your results in No. 11 of this assignment with your results in No. 6. Explain the differences in the Current Text results and the Original Pronouncements results.

        _____

        _____

        _____

        _____

Exercise 4-3   Name: _____
Understanding the Contents of the Infobases Section: _____

1.   Open the Current Text. Using the Query button on the toolbelt, query the term *gains*
      —how many hits do you find?

      _____

2.   Look at the third line of the reference window. List the first cite found in the Current
      Text for the query *gains*.

      _____

3.   In what order do the Current Text cites appear?

      _____

      _____

4.   Scroll down through the text of the results on your search in the Current Text. Do you
      see any superseded material (shaded text) in your results? If so, identify one superseded
      paragraph.

      _____

5.   Page down to the record that contains the cite C11.102 in the Current Text. Notice the
      cross-referencing at the end of the paragraph in brackets. What is the reference number?

      _____

6.   Copy the paragraph from C11.102. How many lines of text are shown on the screen?
      What does the jump link reference in this record?

      _____

      _____

7.   Open the Original Pronouncements. Search for the term *gains*—how many cites do you
      find?

      _____

8.   What is the first cite you found in the Original Pronouncements?

      _____

9.   In what order are your results found in the Original Pronouncements?

_____

_____

10.   Scroll down through the text of the results on your search for *gains* in the Original
        Pronouncements. Do you find any superseded material? If so, cite one superseded
        paragraph.

        _____

11.   Page down to the record that contains the cite APB 29, Par. 28. How many lines of text
        are shown on the screen?

        _____

12.   Using the pop-up link to view the footnote contained in APB 29, Par. 28, copy the
        footnote in the space provided.

_____

_____

_____

_____

13.   Compare your results in No. 11 of this assignment with your results in No. 6. Explain the
        differences in the Current Text results and the Original Pronouncements results.

_____

_____

_____

_____

Exercise 4-4   Name: _____
Understanding Infobase Results   Section: _____

1.   Open the Original Pronouncements and query *inventory*—how many hits do you find?

      _____

2.   List the cites for the first four records that contain the term *inventory*.

      _____   _____

      _____   _____

3.   List the cites for the first four standards that contain the term *inventory*.

      _____   _____

      _____   _____

4.   Explain the difference between a record and a standard.

      _____

      _____

      _____

      _____

Exercise 4-5   Name: _____
Understanding Infobase Results   Section: _____

1.   Open the Original Pronouncements and query *land*—how many hits do you find?

        _____

2.   List the cites for the first four records that contain the term *land*.

        _____   _____

        _____   _____

3.   List the cites for the first four standards that contain the term *land*.

        _____   _____

        _____   _____

4.   Explain the difference between a record and a standard.

        _____

        _____

        _____

        _____

Exercise 4 -6   Name: _____

Understanding Infobase Results   Section: _____

1.   Open the Original Pronouncements and query *amortization*—how many hits do you find?

       _____

2.   List the cites for the first four records that contain the term *amortization*.

       _____   _____

       _____   _____

3.   List the cites for the first four standards that contain the term *amortization*.

       _____   _____

       _____   _____

4.   Explain the difference between a record and a standard.

_____

_____

_____

_____

Exercise 4-7　　　　　　　　　Name: _____
Understanding Queries　　　　Section: _____

1.　　Using the Original Pronouncements, search for the term *dividend*. How many hits do you find?

　　　　_____

2.　　List the first four records where the term *dividend* is found.

　　　　_____　　　　　_____

　　　　_____　　　　　_____

3.　　List the first three standards where the term *dividend* is found.

　　　　_____　　　　　_____

　　　　_____

4.　　Using the Original Pronouncements, search for the term *dividends* (plural). How many hits do you find?

　　　　_____

5.　　List the first four records where the term *dividends* is found.

　　　　_____　　　　　_____

　　　　_____　　　　　_____

6.　　List the first three standards where the term *dividends* is found.

　　　　_____　　　　　_____

　　　　_____

7.　　Why do the searches for the terms *dividend* and *dividends* produce different results in the Original Pronouncements?

_____

_____

Exercise 4-8   Name: _____

Understanding Queries   Section: _____

1.   Using the Original Pronouncements, search for the term *asset*. How many hits do you
      find?

      _____

2.   List the first four records where the term *asset* is found.

      _____   _____

      _____   _____

3.   List the first three standards where the term *asset* is found.

      _____   _____

      _____

4.   Using the Original Pronouncements, search for the term *assets* (plural). How many hits
      do you find?

      _____

5.   List the first four records where the term *assets* is found.

      _____   _____

      _____   _____

6.   List the first three standards where the term *assets* is found.

      _____   _____

      _____

7.   Why do the searches for the terms and *assets* produce different results in the Original
      Pronouncements?

      _____

      _____

      _____

Exercise 4-9   Name: _____
Understanding Queries   Section: _____

1.   Using the Original Pronouncements, search for the term *trademark*. How many hits do you find?

    _____

2.   List the first four records where the term *trademark* is found.

    _____   _____

    _____   _____

3.   List the first three standards where the term *trademark* is found.

    _____   _____

    _____

4.   Using the Original Pronouncements, search for the term *trademarks* (plural). How many hits do you find?

    _____

5.   List the first four records where the term *trademarks* is found.

    _____   _____

    _____   _____

6.   List the first three standards where the term *trademarks* is found.

    _____   _____

    _____

7.   Why do the searches for the terms *trademark* and *trademarks* produce different results in the Original Pronouncements?

    _____

    _____

    _____

Exercise 4-10   Name: _____

Understanding Queries   Section: _____

1.   Using the Original Pronouncements, search for the term *expense*. How many hits do you find?

   _____

2.   List the first four records where the term *expense* is found.

   _____   _____

   _____   _____

3.   List the first three standards where the term *expense* is found.

   _____   _____

   _____

4.   Using the Original Pronouncements, search for the term *expenses* (plural). How many hits do you find?

   _____

5.   List the first four records where the term *expenses* is found.

   _____   _____

   _____   _____

6.   List the first three standards where the term *expenses* is found.

   _____   _____

   _____

7.   Why do the searches for the terms *expense* and *expenses* produce different results in the Original Pronouncements?

   _____

   _____

   _____

Exercise 4-11   Name: _____

Understanding Keywords and Queries   Section: _____

1.   Open the Original Pronouncements and search for the term *debt*. How many hits do you find?

      _____

2.   List the first four records where the term *debt* appears.

      _____   _____

      _____   _____

3.   List the first four standards where the term *debt* appears.

      _____   _____

      _____   _____

4.   Open the Original Pronouncements and search for the term *liability*. How many hits do you find?

      _____

5.   List the first four records where the term *liability* appears.

      _____   _____

      _____   _____

6.   List the first four standards where the term *liability* appears.

      _____   _____

      _____   _____

7.   If the words *debt* and *liability* have the same meaning in accounting, why are your search results different for these two terms?

      _____

      _____

      _____

Exercise 4-12   Name: _____

Understanding Keywords and Queries   Section: _____

1.   Open the Original Pronouncements and search for the term *shareholder*. How many hits do you find?

_____

2.   List the first four records where the term *shareholder* appears.

_____   _____

_____   _____

3.   List the first four standards where the term *shareholder* appears.

_____   _____

_____   _____

4.   Open the Original Pronouncements and search for the term *stockholder*. How many hits do you find?

_____

5.   List the first four records where the term *stockholder* appears.

_____   _____

_____   _____

6.   List the first four standards where the term *stockholder* appears.

_____   _____

_____   _____

7.   If the words *shareholder* and *stockholder* have the same meaning in accounting, why are your search results different for these two terms?

_____

_____

_____

Exercise 4-13   Name: _____

Understanding Keywords and Queries   Section: _____

1.   Open the Original Pronouncements and search for the term *sales*. How many hits do you find?

      _____

2.   List the first four records where the term *sales* appears.

      _____   _____

      _____   _____

3.   List the first four standards where the term *sales* appears.

      _____   _____

      _____   _____

4.   Open the Original Pronouncements and search for the term *revenue*. How many hits do you find?

      _____

5.   List the first four records where the term *revenue* appears.

      _____   _____

      _____   _____

6.   List the first four standards where the term *revenue* appears.

      _____   _____

      _____   _____

7.   If the words *sales* and *revenue* have the same meaning in accounting, why are your search results different for these two terms?

_____

_____

_____

SEARCH AND RETRIEVAL TECHNIQUES

Search Operators

Locating the appropriate literature for a given case requires a carefully planned and exhaustive search. As we discussed in the previous section, the infobase software searches by keyword rather than subject or topic. Therefore, to be effective in your research, your query must contain the appropriate keywords. Search operators and multiple keywords used effectively will expand or narrow the scope of your search.

The table below shows five logic operators that can be used to narrow or expand your search.

Logic Operators

*	Wildcard
&	And
|	Or
^	Not
~	Exclusive Or

The WILDCARD Operator. The asterisk or * symbol is used as a wildcard to expand your search to various forms of the word. For example, if you typed in the query box *depreciati**, the results would include all records that contained the terms beginning with *depreciati*, which would include *depreciating*, *depreciation*, and *depreciation*. It would not include records that contained the term *depreciate* or *depreciable*. If you wanted to find those records, you would use the wildcard earlier in the search string and type *deprecia**. Monitoring the word box will assist you in deciding where you can most effectively place the wildcard.

The AND Operator. The AND operator narrows your search. It locates all records that contain both terms. For example, if you searched for the string *fixed & assets*, you would find all records that contained both the terms *fixed* and *assets* in the same record. We can activate the AND operator in three ways: by placing an ampersand & sign in between the search terms, by typing the word AND between the two search terms, or by leaving a blank space between the two search terms. (A space between words defaults to the AND operator.) Conceptualizing the results of this search by using a Venn diagram is easy.

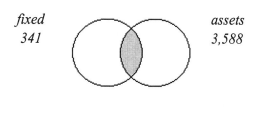

fixed   *assets*
341   *3,588*

fixed & assets
108

The query window and search results for the AND operator are shown in Exhibit 4-13.

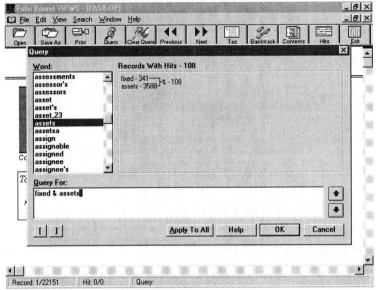

EXHIBIT 4-13

The results window shows that there are 341 records that contain the term *fixed* and 3,588 records that contain the term *assets*. There are 108 records that contain both the terms *fixed* and *assets* in the same record. The AND logic operator is a powerful tool for narrowing your search to find records with both terms. In this example we have narrowed the term *assets* from 3,588 records down to 341 records. We have most likely ruled out records that discuss current assets or any record that generically discusses assets.

The OR Logic Operator. The OR logic operator is activated by using the | symbol or typing the word OR between the search terms. This expands the search and looks for all records where either term is found.   Exhibit 4-14 displays the search results for the query *fixed | assets*.

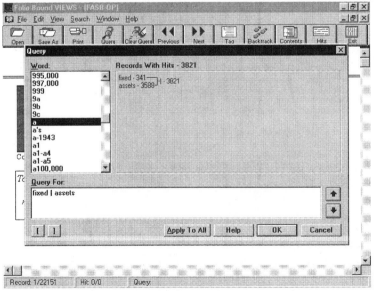

EXHIBIT 4-14

The results window shows there are 341 records with the term *fixed* and 3,588 with the term *assets*. At first glance, you might think that searching for either term would produce 341 + 3,588 = 3,929 records. However, there were 108 records where both terms were found together. If we added the number of records for each word together, this would double count the 108 records where the two terms are found together. The Venn diagram below depicts the results of this search.

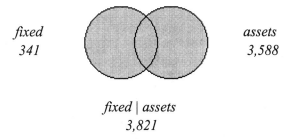

fixed
341

assets
3,588

fixed | assets
3,821

Mathematically, we would then expect the following number of hits for the query *fixed | assets:*

$$341 + 3,588 - 108 = 3,821$$

The results windows verifies this solution. Because the OR operator searches for all places where either word is found, the OR operator expands your search.

The NOT Logic Operator. The karat symbol $^\wedge$ or the word NOT is used to exclude a search term. For example, if you would like to look for all the records with the term *fixed* but not the term *assets*, you would use the following query:

fixed $^\wedge$ assets
fixed NOT assets

A conceptual view of this search using a Venn diagram is shown below:

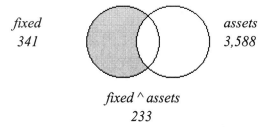

fixed
341

assets
3,588

fixed $^\wedge$ assets
233

The overlap or intersection where the terms *fixed* and *assets* are found together is 108. Therefore, we would expect to find 341 - 108 = 233 records where the term *fixed* is found without the term *assets*.

An important point to notice with the NOT operator (^) is that this operator is not commutative in nature. In other words, the order of operations matters. The query *assets ^ fixed* would search for all places where the term *assets* is found without the term *fixed* and would produce dramatically different results, 3,480 hits. The query *assets ^ fixed* is conceptually shown below.

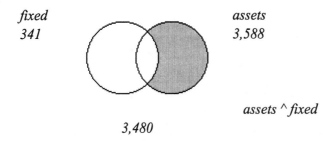

Exhibit 4-15 confirms there are 3,480 hits to the query *assets ^ fixed*.

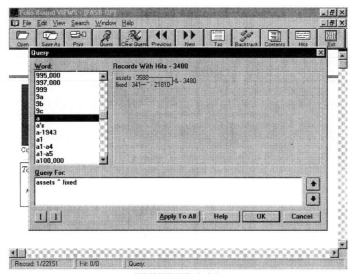

EXHIBIT 4-15

The EXCLUSIVE OR Operator. The tilde symbol ~ or the operator XOR is used to broaden the search and look for all places where either term is found but excludes the records in which they are found together. This is easiest seen by the Venn diagram below:

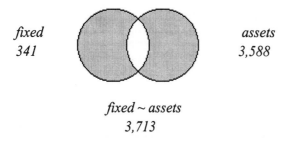

Again, mathematically, we can see the results of the search:

Records containing the term *fixed* and not *assets*   233
Records containing the term *assets* and not *fixed* <u>3,480</u>

Records containing either term *fixed* or *assets*
but not records where they are found together   3,713

The results window in Exhibit 4-16 confirms our logic as shown below.

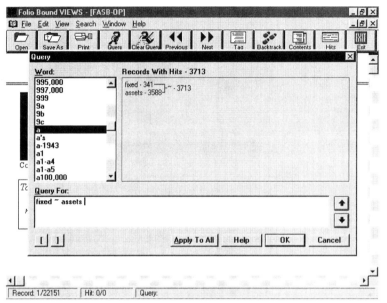

EXHIBIT 4-16

If you analyze the Venn diagram, you will notice that the EXCLUSIVE OR ~ operator will produce the same results for either query *fixed* ~ *assets* or *assets* ~ *fixed*. Therefore, the ordering of search terms when using this logic operator is not important.

A brief review of the diagrams, the logic operators, and the results are shown below:

Review of Logic Operators

Fixed & assets	108	
Assets & fixed	108	
Fixed | assets	3,821	
Assets | fixed	3,821	
Fixed ^ assets	233	
Assets ^ Fixed	3,480	
Fixed ~ assets	3,713	
Assets ~ fixed	3,713	

Character String Searches, Proximity Searches, and Nested Searches

Character String Searches. A powerful way to narrow your search is by searching for exact matches of several words together. Quotation marks are placed around the terms to indicate an exact character string search. For example, if you wanted to search for all records where the words *fixed assets* are found not just in the same record, but you want the two words together, you would type in the following query:

"fixed assets"

Exhibit 4-17 contains the results window for the character string search:

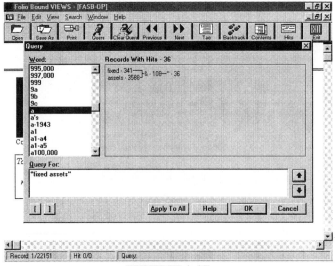

EXHIBIT 4-17

Notice the character string search produced only 36 records. Compare this result with the first query in which we searched for all records where the terms *fixed* and *assets* were found in the same record, but not necessarily together. The search with the & operator produced 108 hits. The use of quotations to produce an exact match of a multiple-word character string narrows your search considerably.

Proximity Searches. Another way to narrow your search is to use a proximity search. Proximity searches search for two terms but only within the specified number of words of each other. In addition, proximity searches are either "ordered" or "unordered" proximity searches.

An ordered proximity search looks for the two terms in that specific order. Quotation marks are placed around the two terms, which makes the query look like a character string search. However, when you place the slash sign and a number /5 at the end of the quotation marks, the infobase searches for all places where the two words are found within five words of each other. You can place any number at the end of the proximity search. A larger number expands the search; a smaller number narrows the search.

Suppose we wanted to narrow our search and find all records that contained the terms *fixed* and *assets* in the same folio within ten words of each other. We would type in the following query:

"fixed assets"/10

This query produced 45 records. In most of the records, the terms *fixed* and *assets* were found together because the two terms together are normal accounting vocabulary. However, as shown in record 34/45 below, there are instances in the infobase where *fixed* and *assets* are in the same folio but are not found together. Exhibit 4-18 shows records 34 and 35 of our ordered proximity search:

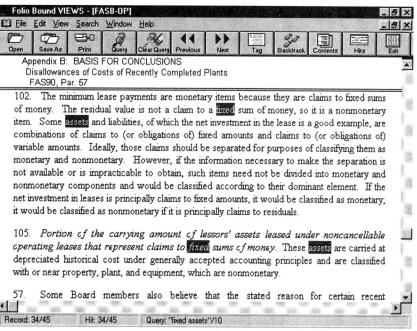

EXHIBIT 4-18

Note that the term *fixed* is always found first and the term *assets* is found within 10 words AFTER the word *fixed*.   This is called an ordered proximity search because it searches for the two terms in that order.

An unordered proximity search looks for the two terms within the designated number of words of each other in either order. If we wanted to look for wherever the terms *fixed* and *assets* were found together within ten words of each other in either order, we would use the following query:

"fixed assets"@10

This will produce records where the word *assets* is found before the term *fixed*, which will slightly broaden your search. Compare the results window in Exhibit 4-19 with the previous results window using an ordered proximity search. Notice that in some folios the word *fixed* appears first, and in other folios the word *asset* appears first.

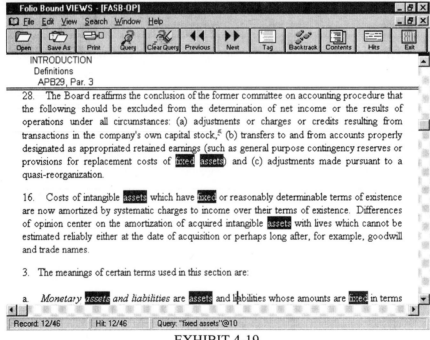

EXHIBIT 4-19

Nested Searches. The infobase allows you to use parentheses to define the order of operations in a search string. The infobase views these parentheses in the same manner as the mathematical order of operations.   The infobase solves the portion of the search within the parentheses first, and then the order of operations is from left to right. Where there are more than two search terms and no parentheses are used, the order of operations is the same as in mathematics, from left to right.

Below are the results of two searches that use parentheses. Notice the dramatic difference in the search results by changing the location of the parentheses.

Query #1	(fixed & assets) | depreciation	693 records
Query #2	fixed & (assets | depreciation)	115 records

It is easiest to depict these differences using a results diagram.

Query #1   (fixed & assets) | depreciation

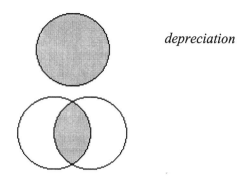

fixed & assets

The first query *(fixed & assets) | depreciation* finds all records that contain both the terms *fixed* and *assets* (the intersection) or the term *depreciation*. The infobase then looks for all places where the term *depreciation* is found anywhere within the infobase. Since the OR operator was used, all records containing *depreciation* are included in the hits.

Query #2   fixed & (assets | depreciation)

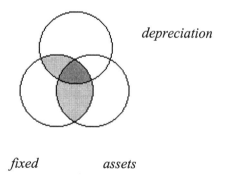

fixed   *assets*

The second query *fixed & (asset | depreciation)* searches for any record where either term *assets* or *depreciation* is found, and then takes those results and looks for the intersection with the term *fixed*. In essence, this is the equivalent of searching for *fixed & assets* and combining those results with the results of *fixed & depreciation.*

Notice how dramatically different the search results are between Queries #1 and #2 merely by changing the nesting. We must pay careful attention to logic operators and nesting in order to locate the appropriate authority when conducting research.

Search Tips

To understand when each type of search is appropriate, it is helpful to compare and contrast the different queries. In the previous section we had searched for all places where *fixed* and *assets* were found in the same record, which produced 108 records. As you can see from reading the contents of some of those records, some of the records pertained to the accounting concept or classification of a fixed asset, but other records merely happened to have those two words within the record. Therefore, the AND search produced more material that is irrelevant to research on the subject of fixed assets.

The character string search was extremely narrow and searched only for where the two terms were found together (36 hits). The ordered proximity searched for records where the word *fixed* preceded the word *assets*, but the two words were within ten words of each other. The ordered proximity search, therefore, broadened our character string search but narrowed it from the & search. The unordered proximity looked for the terms in either order, which again slightly broadened our search compared to a character string search.

Two interesting points should be made regarding our queries on fixed assets. The first issue is that if we were interested in the subject of fixed assets, the unordered proximity that produces records where the words *assets* and *fixed* in a backward order might not be an appropriate search. The second point is that by using the terms *fixed* and *assets*, we have limited ourselves to the plural form of the word, which effectively eliminates all records that contained the terms *fixed asset* (singular).

Effective research requires an exhaustive search in the professional literature. Therefore, it would probably be more appropriate to search for *fixed asset** when using the &, |, ^, or ~ logic operators. However, since a wildcard is not acceptable in a proximity search (it looks for exact characters), you would need to perform two ordered proximity searches: one for *"fixed asset"/10* and anoter for *"fixed assets"/10*.

Which search string is best? It depends on the particular research question you are addressing. Your first attempts in research and search queries may be frustrating and time-consuming. However, the more practice you have with developing search queries and searching, the easier and faster you will become in your research. Patience and experience with the infobase will help you become an efficient and effective researcher.

Exercise 4-14   Name: _____

Understanding Search Operators   Section: _____

Instructions: Use the Original Pronouncements infobase to search the following queries. Shade the Venn diagram to depict the results of each search and label the diagram with the number of hits found.

1.   consolidated

2.   income

3.   consolidated & income

4.   income ^ consolidated

5.   consolidated ~ income

6.   consolidated ^ income

7.   income | consolidated

8.   consolidated income

Exercise 4-15   Name: _____
Understanding Search Operators   Section: _____

Instructions: Use the Original Pronouncements infobase to search the following queries. Shade the Venn diagram to depict the results of each search and label the diagram with the number of hits found.

1.   discontinued

2.   operations

3.   discontinued ^ operations

4.   operations | discontinued

5.   discontinued & operations

6.   discontinued ~ operations

7.   operations ^ discontinued

8.   discontinued | operations

Exercise 4-16   Name: _____
Understanding Search Operators   Section: _____

Instructions: Use the Original Pronouncements infobase to search the following queries.
Shade the Venn diagram to depict the results of each search and label the diagram with the
number of hits found.

1.   intangible

2.   asset

3.   intangible | asset

4.   intangible ^ asset

5.   intangible & asset

6.   intangible ~ asset

7.   asset ^ intangible

8.   asset ~ intangible

Exercise 4-17   Name: _____

Understanding Search Operators   Section: _____

Instructions: Use the Original Pronouncements infobase to search the following queries. Shade the Venn diagram to depict the results of each search and label the diagram with the number of hits found.

1.   preferred

2.   stock

3.   preferred ~ stock

4.   preferred stock

5.   preferred ^ stock

6.   stock | preferred

7.   stock ~ preferred

8.   stock ^ preferred

Exercise 4-18   Name: _____

Understanding Search Results   Section: _____

Instructions: Below is the results window for a given query. Using these results, calculate the
number of hits you would expect to find for each of the following search strings.

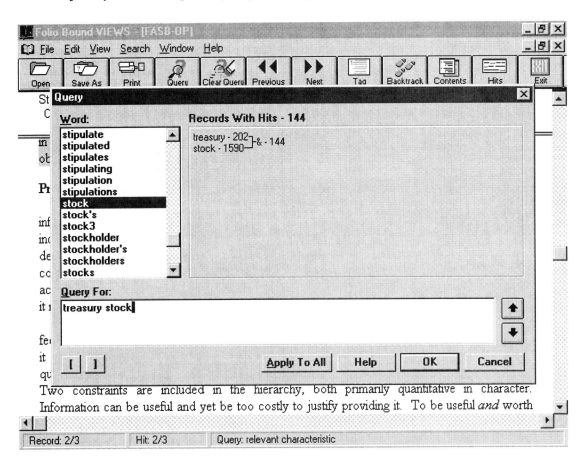

1.   stock ^ treasury   _____

2.   treasury | stock   _____

3.   treasury ^ stock   _____

4.   treasury ~ stock   _____

5.   stock | treasury   _____

Exercise 4-19   Name: _____
Understanding Search Results   Section: _____

Instructions: Below is the results window for a given query. Using these results, calculate the number of hits you would expect to find for each of the following search strings.

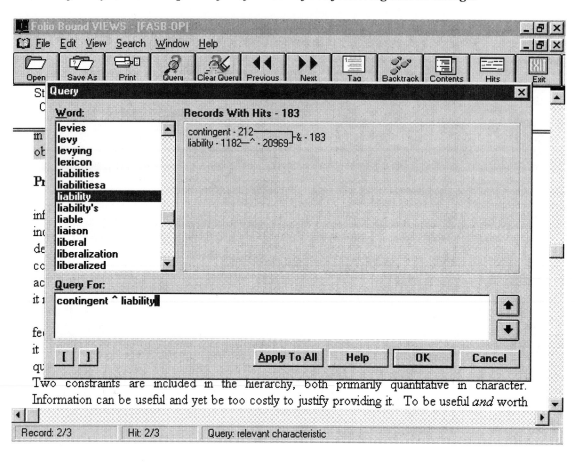

1.   contingent & liability   _____

2.   liability ^ contingent   _____

3.   liability | contingent   _____

4.   contingent ^ liability   _____

5.   liability ~ contingent   _____

Exercise 4-20
Understanding Search Results

Name: _____

Section: _____

Instructions: Below is the results window for a given query. Using these results, calculate the number of hits you would expect to find for each of the following search strings.

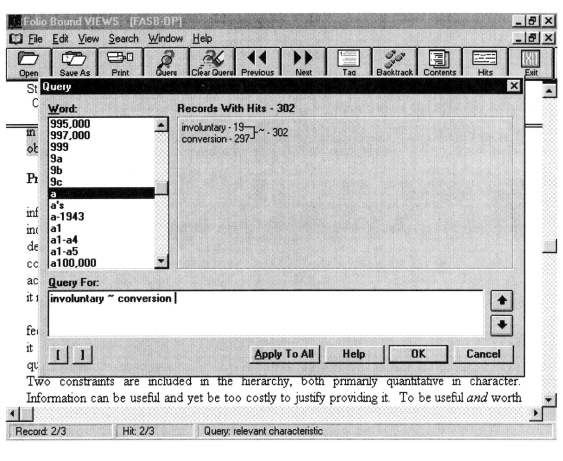

1.   involuntary & conversion   _____

2.   involuntary ^ conversion   _____

3.   involuntary | conversion   _____

4.   conversion ~ involuntary   _____

5.   conversion ^ involuntary   _____

Exercise 4-21   Name: _____
Understanding Search Results   Section: _____

Instructions: Below is the results window for a given query. Using these results, calculate the number of hits you would expect to find for each of the following search strings.

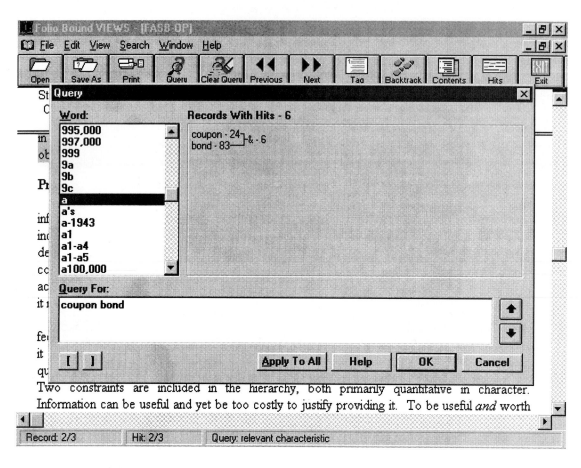

1.   bond ^ coupon   _____

2.   bond | coupon   _____

3.   bond coupon   _____

4.   coupon ~ bond   _____

5.   coupon ^ bond   _____

Exercise 4-22   Name: _____
Developing Search Queries   Section: _____

Instructions: You would like to search for the following information. Develop the query you would use to accomplish each search. Search for those terms in the Original Pronouncements and indicate the number of hits you find for each query.

		Query	**Hits**
1.	All records where the terms *revenue* and *recognition* are found within ten words are found in either direction.	_____	___
2.	All records where the term *revenue* is found without the term *recognition*.	_____	___
3.	All records where either term *revenue* or *recognition* is found.	_____	___
4.	All records where *recognition* is found without the term *revenue*.	_____	___
5.	All records where *recognition* and *revenue* are found, but not where they are found in the same record.	_____	___
6.	All records where the subject of revenue recognition can be found.	_____	___
7.	All records where the two words *revenue* and *recognition* are found written together with no words in between.	_____	___
8.	All records where the terms *revenue* and *recognition* are found in the same record.	_____	___

Exercise 4-23   Name: _____
Developing Search Queries   Section: _____

Instructions: You would like to search for the following information. Develop the query you would use to accomplish each search. Search for those terms in the Original Pronouncements and indicate the number of hits you find for each query.

	Query	Hits
1. All records where the two words *stock* and *rights* are found together with no words in between.	_____	____
2. All records where the term *stock* is found without the word *rights*.	_____	____
3. All records where the subject of stock rights can be found.	_____	____
4. All records where the term *rights* is found without the term *stock*.	_____	____
5. All records where either the term *stock* or the term *rights* is found.	_____	____
6. All records where the terms *stock* and *rights* are found in the same record.	_____	____
7. All records where the terms *stock* and *rights* are found within five words of each other in that order.	_____	____
8. All records where *stock* and *rights* can be found but not where they are in the same record.	_____	____

Exercise 4-24   Name: _____
Developing Search Queries   Section: _____

Instructions: You would like to search for the following information. Develop the query would use to accomplish each search. Search for those terms in the Original Pronouncements and indicate the number of hits you find for each query.

	Query	**Hits**
1. All records where the term *capital* is found without the term *lease*.	_____	___
2. All records where the terms *capital* and *lease* are found together.	_____	___
3. All records where *capital* and *lease* are found, but not where they are found in the same record.	_____	___
4. All records where the two words *capital* and *lease* are found together with no words in between.	_____	___
5. All records where the term *lease* is found without the term *capital*.	_____	___
6. All records where the terms *capital* and *lease* are found within eight words of each other in any order.	_____	___
7. All records that contain information on the topic of a capital lease.	_____	___
8. All records that contain either the term *capital* or the term *lease*.	_____	___

Exercise 4-25
Developing Search Queries

Name: _____

Section: _____

Instructions: You would like to search for the following information. Develop the query you would use to accomplish each search. Search for those terms in the Original Pronouncements and indicate the number of hits you find for each query.

		Query	Hits
1.	All records where the term *income* is found without the term *tax*.	_____	____
2.	All records where the terms *income* and *tax* are found in the same records within five words of each other in that order.	_____	____
3.	All records that contain either the term *income* or the term *tax*.	_____	____
4.	All records that have the two words *income* and *tax* found together with no words in between.	_____	____
5.	All records that contain both the terms *income* and *tax*.	_____	____
6.	All records that contain the term *tax* without the term *income*.	_____	____
7.	All records that contain information on the subject of income tax.	_____	____
8.	All records where either the term *income* or *tax* is found, but not where they are found in the same record.	_____	____

Exercise 4-26   Name: _____
Developing Search Strings   Section: _____

Issue: What are the options a company has for recognizing revenue when it sells to customers
         on contract?

1.   Generate a query. _____

2.   What is the number of hits found? _____

3.   Cite the first four records found.

         a) _____

         b) _____

         c) _____

         d) _____

4.   Read the four cites above. Mark each cite as to whether it applies to the issue.

         a)   applies   does not apply

         b)   applies   does not apply

         c)   applies   does not apply

         d)   applies   does not apply

5.   Generate three additional queries that may locate the appropriate authority.

                 _____

                 _____

                 _____

Exercise 4-27   Name: _____
Developing Search Strings   Section: _____

Issue: A company has customers who have delinquent accounts. What alternatives does the
         company have in accounting for this situation?

1.   Generate a query. _____

2.   What is the number of hits found? _____

3.   Cite the first four records found.

         a) _____

         b) _____

         c) _____

         d) _____

4.   Read the four cites above. Mark each cite as to whether it applies to the issue.

         a)   applies   does not apply

         b)   applies   does not apply

         c)   applies   does not apply

         d)   applies   does not apply

5.   Generate three additional queries that may locate the appropriate authority.

                 _____

                 _____

                 _____

Exercise 4-28   Name: _____
Developing Search Strings   Section: _____

Issue: A company is trying to determine how to value the inventory that is produced in its
         factory.

1.   Generate a query. _____

2.   What is the number of hits found? _____

3.   Cite the first four records found.

         a) _____

         b) _____

         c) _____

         d) _____

4.   Read the four cites above. Mark each cite as to whether it applies to the issue.

         a)   applies   does not apply

         b)   applies   does not apply

         c)   applies   does not apply

         d)   applies   does not apply

5.   Generate three additional queries that may locate the appropriate authority.

         _____

         _____

         _____

Exercise 4-29   **Name:** _____

Developing Search Strings   **Section:** _____

Issue: A company is trying to determine whether an investment in 100 shares of stock should be disclosed as a current asset.

1.   Generate a query. _____

2.   What is the number of hits found? _____

3.   Cite the first four records found.

        a) _____

        b) _____

        c) _____

        d) _____

4.   Read the four cites above. Mark each cite as to whether it applies to the issue.

        a)   applies   does not apply

        b)   applies   does not apply

        c)   applies   does not apply

        d)   applies   does not apply

5.   Generate three additional queries that may locate the appropriate authority.

                _____

                _____

                _____

Exercise 4-30 Name: _____

Generating Keywords Section: _____

Accounting vocabulary often uses synonyms. For example, the balance sheet is also referred to as the statement of financial position. This exercise will strengthen your ability to generate additional keywords for a given topic.

1. List as many synonyms as you can for *fixed assets*.

    _____   _____

    _____   _____

    _____   _____

    _____   _____

2. Develop a query for two of the synonyms listed above. Complete the table below showing the number of records found for each query and cite the first three records for each query.

Query	Hits	Cites
"fixed assets"	_____	1. _____
		2. _____
		3. _____
_____	_____	1. _____
		2. _____
		3. _____
_____	_____	1. _____
		2. _____
		3. _____

Exercise 4-31   Name: _____
Generating Keywords   Section: _____

Accounting vocabulary often uses synonyms. For example, the balance sheet is also referred to as the statement of financial position. This exercise will strengthen your ability to generate additional keywords for a given topic.

1.   List as many synonyms as you can for *debt*.

      _____   _____

      _____   _____

      _____   _____

      _____   _____

2.   Develop a query for two of the synonyms listed above. Complete the table below showing the number of records found for each query and cite the first three records for each query.

Query	Hits	Cites
"debt"	_____	1. _____
		2. _____
		3. _____
_____	_____	1. _____
		2. _____
		3. _____
_____	_____	1. _____
		2. _____
		3. _____

Exercise 4-32   Name: _____
Generating Keywords   Section: _____

Accounting vocabulary often uses synonyms. For example, the balance sheet is also referred to as the statement of financial position. This exercise will strengthen your ability to generate additional keywords for a given topic.

1.   List as many synonyms as you can for *bad debts*.

      _____   _____

      _____   _____

      _____   _____

      _____   _____

2.   Develop a query for two of the synonyms listed above. Complete the table below showing the number of records found for each query and cite the first three records for each query.

Query	Hits	Cites
"bad debts"	_____	1. _____
		2. _____
		3. _____
_____	_____	1. _____
		2. _____
		3. _____
_____	_____	1. _____
		2. _____
		3. _____

Exercise 4-33   Name: _____

Generating Keywords   Section: _____

Accounting vocabulary often uses synonyms. For example, the balance sheet is also referred to as the statement of financial position. This exercise will strengthen your ability to generate additional keywords for a given topic.

1.   List as many synonyms as you can for *capital stock*.

       _____   _____

       _____   _____

       _____   _____

       _____   _____

2.   Develop a query for two of the synonyms listed above. Complete the table below showing the number of records found for each query and cite the first three records for each query.

Query	Hits	Cites
"capital stock"	_____	1. _____
		2. _____
		3. _____
_____	_____	1. _____
		2. _____
		3. _____
_____	_____	1. _____
		2. _____
		3. _____

THE RESEARCH PROCESS

The research process includes the following five steps:

1. Defining the problem.
2. Developing keywords and searching the infobase.
3. Critically evaluating the literature.
4. Downloading and printing the appropriate literature.
5. Writing the research report.

Becoming very involved and bogged down with a particular piece of research is easy. As you can see from the size and complexity of the infobase, going in circles would be easy, reading and rereading the same cites. To be an efficient and effective researcher, you must locate all applicable cites. In other words, your search should be exhaustive. Therefore, the strength of your research capabilities will be in generating the most effective keywords and tracking your results.

Finding the Appropriate Literature

Reading technical material is challenging because it is written at a relatively high reading level. The sentences can often be lengthy and difficult to comprehend. Because the infobase searches for character strings and not topics, your search will often include many records that are unrelated to your research topic. Finding the appropriate literature is easier if you follow these basic research strategies.

1. Keep a record or log of your keywords. As you search, check them off, indicating the number of hits you find on each search.

2. Skim the records looking for two things: items that are on point and hints for additional keywords. As you read and develop more ideas on the topic, generate new keywords and add them to the bottom of your list.

3. Change the settings on your reference window to better help you in your search. For example, a one-line reference window gives you more text on your screen and makes reading and scrolling through the document faster. A three-line reference window shows the title or topic and may help you discern that the particular record is not on point.

4. When you find materials that you think may be on point, you can highlight and copy those records, or you can tag them and save them to a file.

5. Performing multiple queries and toggling between the queries will save time and energy.

6. Viewing the table of contents of your search results to find applicable standards may narrow your search. The table of contents will also allow you to read applicable standards in their entirety.

Viewing Search Results

When you type in your query and click the return key twice, the window displays the full text of the results. Although your keyword may appear in the record several times, the paragraph retrieved counts as one record. You can move from highlighted word to the next highlighted word by pressing the F3 key or hitting "Next" on the toolbelt. You can move backward to the previous highlighted word by pressing F4 or "Previous" on the toolbelt.

Suppose we queried *coupon bond.* The first results window is shown in Exhibit 4-20.

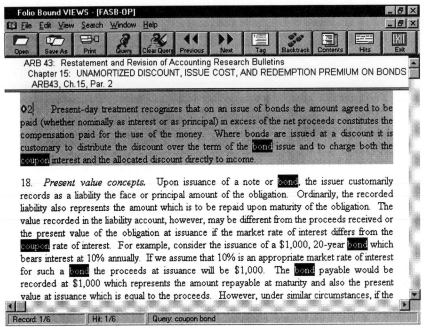

EXHIBIT 4-20

Notice the numbers in the bottom left-hand corner of the window. When you are looking at the results of your search, the infobase shows you that you are in record #1 of 6 records, that you are in hit #1 of 6 hits, and the query is *coupon bond.*

When viewing your results, having three items checked on the View pull-down menu, as shown in Exhibit 4-21, is helpful.

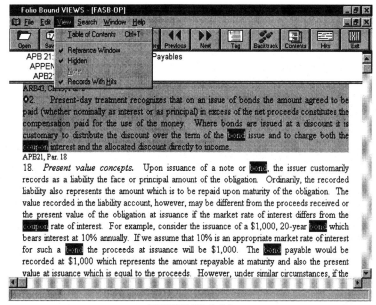

EXHIBIT 4-21

The "Reference Window" setting indicates whether the reference window is present. The default setting for the reference window is three lines. The first line shows the standard, the second line the chapter and title, and the third line the citation. The citation in the third line indicates the standard, chapter (if applicable), and paragraph of the pronouncement in which your cursor is positioned.

To adjust the number of lines in the reference window, you must change the default settings. Normally it is helpful to have at least three lines displayed. However, if you are trying to read as much text as possible on the screen, changing the reference window setting to one line will display only the citation line. To change the settings, you must use the "File" command and access the "Preferences" menu, as shown in Exhibit 4-22.

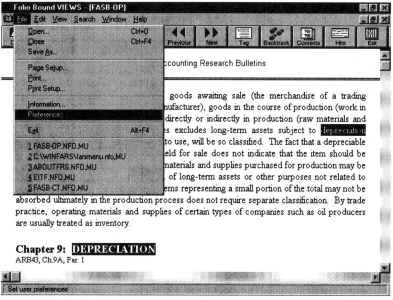

EXHIBIT 4-22

Click on "Preferences" to change the reference window settings. The menu in Exhibit 4-23 will appear:

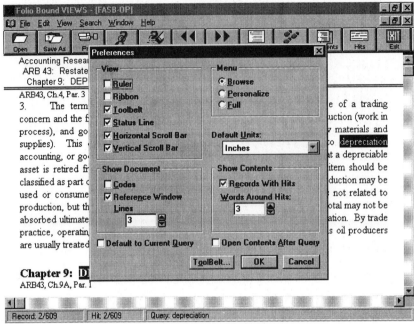

EXHIBIT 4-23

In the lower left-hand corner under "Show Document," the check-mark next to Reference Window activates the reference window. Leave this item checked, and click on "Lines" to change the number of lines that will show in the reference window. Before you exit the program, be sure to change the setting back to three lines for the next user. If you are working in a laboratory environment or a shared computer environment, **we recommend that you DO NOT change any other default settings.** Changing default settings may alter the shading, highlighting, menus, toolbelts, or results of the infobase that could affect your research results.

The second item to have checked on the View command is the setting "Hidden. " Checking Hidden places the standard number and citation in blue highlights in the space above the record. Compare our first screen capture for *coupon bond* (Exhibit 4-20) with the second screen capture (Exhibit 4-21). In Exhibit 4-20, you will see a blank line between the records; in Exhibit 4-21, the cite is printed as hidden text in this area. Hidden is an important setting to have activated for downloading and printing purposes.

The third item checked is "Records With Hits." This indicates that you are viewing the full text of the records with all highlighted hits. If we click on "Table of Contents" in this menu, the window changes from the full text of the results to a table of contents of our results. Exhibit 4-24 displays the table of contents for our query for *coupon bond*.

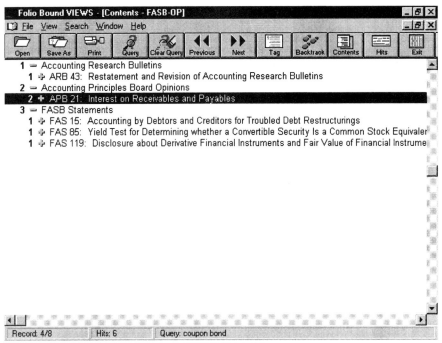

EXHIBIT 4-24

The table of contents for your search results is helpful in conducting research because it lists the types of standard, the standard number, and the number of hits found within each standard. In the query for *coupon bond*, we found a total of six hits: one in the Accounting Research Bulletins, two in the Accounting Principles Board Opinions, and three in the FASB Statements. Notice that the three hits in the FASB Statements are in three different standards. We can sometimes use this information to rule out standards that may not apply to our particular research situation. To view the standard in its entirety, we can either cursor down and double click on the standard, or use the pull-down menu with the "Document" command as shown in Exhibit 4-25.

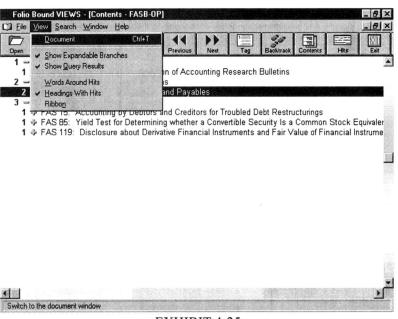

EXHIBIT 4-25

If we retrieve APB 21, which we have highlighted, we will see Exhibit 4-26.

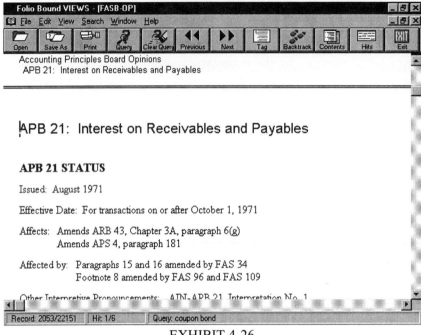

EXHIBIT 4-26

By double clicking on Document or the desired standard in the table of contents list, the standard is retrieved in its entirety. You can now read the standard from start to finish sequentially. When you reach the record that contains the hit from your query, you will notice that the keywords will be highlighted in blue.

When we accessed APB 21 above, notice that the record number has changed to 2053/22151. The record number tracks where this record is in relation to the entire infobase. The hit number still tracks where you are in your search. Here, the window indicates Hit: 1/6. Although we double clicked on the standard for the second hit, this number will not change to 2/6 until we position our cursor in the record of the second hit with the highlighted words *coupon bond.*

Working with Multiple Queries and Views

Searching for several queries during your research session and toggling between the windows is possible. Suppose that we began our research with the query *fixed assets.* We continued our research and searched for depreciation, and then combined the search for *fixed assets* and *depreciation* using various logic operators. We could then toggle between these search results by using the pull-down menu "Search" command as shown in Exhibit 4-27.

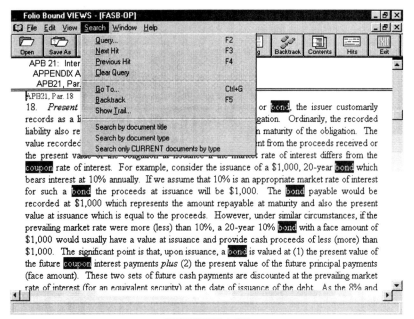

EXHIBIT 4-27

A brief discussion of each Search command is shown below.

Query. Activated through the Search menu. However, the "Query" command is more efficiently activated by using the F2 command using one keystroke.

Next Hit/Previous Hit. As discussed earlier, you can use the menu commands to move to the next hit or previous hit. Using the F3 and F4 keys more efficiently accomplishes this.

Clear Query. Activated through the toolbelt or the search pull-down menu.

Go To. The "Go To" command takes you to a specific record within that query. Control+G activates the "Go To" command from your keyboard.

Backtrack. "Backtrack" is used to go backward one step. Backtrack can also be accomplished with the F5 key. Although backtrack is convenient and takes you back one screen, going forward again is a bit more cumbersome.

Show Trail. The "Show Trail" will allow you to go backward or forward to any query made during the current research session.

Activating the Show Trail command will give you the window displayed in Exhibit 4-28. As you can see from our trail, we have searched for several queries involving fixed assets and depreciation. To view previous query results, double click on the desired query line. The window will change to the results/contents of the selected query.

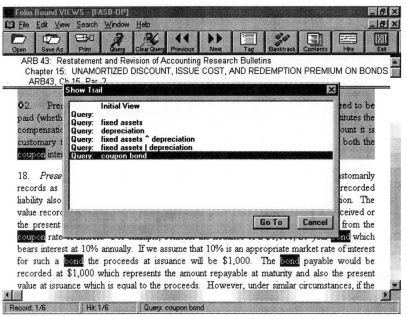

EXHIBIT 4-28

Commands and Hotkeys

A *hotkey* is a function key or set of keystrokes that enables you to activate commands by using the keyboard instead of the mouse. Below is a brief review of the commands and hotkeys available.

Review of Commands and Hotkeys

F1	Help	F2	Query
F3	Next	F4	Previous
F5	Backtrack	Control+G	Go To

Downloading and Printing Records

Several methods can be used to download or print records from the infobase. You can highlight, copy, and paste directly into a word processing document, or you can tag one or more records and save them to a word processing file for later use. The "Edit" command with its pull-down menu allows you to perform these tasks. The "Edit" menu shown in Exhibit 4-29 will change the available tasks based upon where you are in the highlighting or tagging process.

For example, in Exhibit 4-29, we highlighted the record we wanted to save (shown highlighted in black). We could then tag the record to save it in a file, or we can click on the "Copy" command and copy it to an opened word processing document.

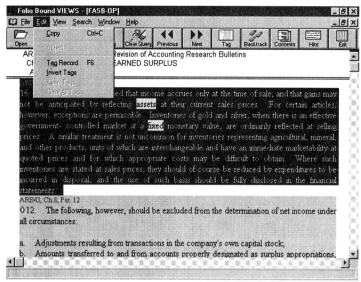

EXHIBIT 4-29

Copy and Paste. To copy and paste records, highlight the record(s) desired, press Edit, and press Copy to put the record into the clipboard. Then click on the minimize box (third box from the right at the top of the screen) to minimize the Folio window. Open up the word processing document, and paste the record(s) into the word processing document. Note that in many cases, the shading, highlighting, and sidebar features that denote superseded text, hits, and amended texts are not maintained when you copy and paste directly from the infobase to the word processing document. Therefore, special care should be taken to note which records are superseded or amended.

Tag Records. To tag a record, you can highlight the record and then click on Edit, and "Tag Record." An easier way to tag records is to have the cursor positioned within the record and click on Edit and Tag Record. A red line will appear to the left side of the tagged record. The menu shown in Exhibit 4-30 lists the various commands for tagging records.

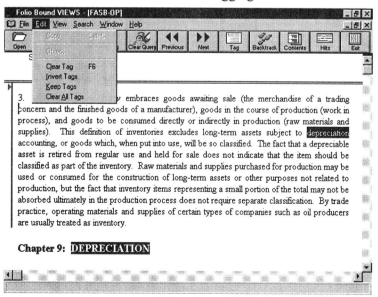

EXHIBIT 4-30

Notice the line (red) to the left of the record with the ▶ symbol that indicates the record has been tagged. You can now activate the "Save" command and save only the records tagged.

Sometimes you would like to save most of the records for a particular query. Rather than tagging every record you would like to save, you can tag the records that you do not want, and then use the "Invert Tags" command to mark those records you do wish to keep.

Save As. To save a file, you can activate the "Save As" command by clicking once on the toolbelt or using the pull-down menu File and Save As. The Save As window will be activated as shown in Exhibit 4-31.

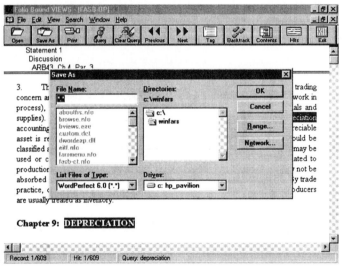

EXHIBIT 4-31

Using the directory window on the right side of the screen, change to the correct drive and directory in which you would like to save your file. Click on the box marked "Range" on the right-hand side of the screen. The menu in Exhibit 4-32 will appear.

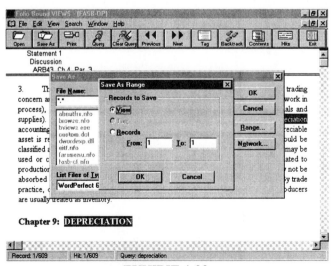

EXHIBIT 4-32

The Range command allows you to save the entire view, tags, or certain records marked in the box next to records (From: To:). Select the item you would like to save (View, Tag, or Records) and click on "OK", which will return you to the Save As main menu. Click on the "List Files of Type" box at the bottom left, and a drop-down menu will appear with the file types as shown in Exhibit 4-33.

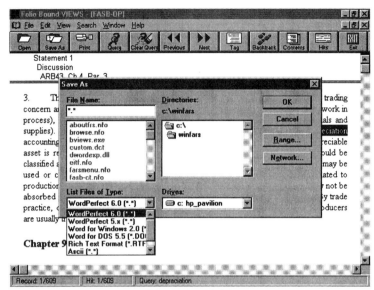

EXHIBIT 4-33

Using the mouse, highlight the desired file type. Then move the mouse to the top left-hand corner marked "File Name" and click. Type in a file name without an extension if you are using WordPerfect. If you are saving the file as a Word document, the file extension will default to doc. Click on OK to save the file.

It is suggested that before tagging or saving records to a file, you check to see that the View menu has the box Hidden checked. This will ensure that the hidden text that contains the citation before each record will be brought into the word processing or ASCII format. The hidden text will be retrieved, provided your word processing program supports hidden text formats and your settings are correct in the word processing program to view and print any hidden text.

Please note that some word processing formats will support the shaded text, hidden text, and marked texts. Recall that superseded text is shaded, and amended text is marked with a bold line to the left-hand side. Since your word processing program may or may not support these features, you should be cautious when downloading records and double-check to be sure you are not citing superseded or amended material.

Advanced Search Commands

Sometimes narrowing your search to a specific area of the infobase is helpful. Querying a certain type of document or a specific document can do this. To perform a query by document title, use the Search command and the pull-down menu as shown in Exhibit 4-34.

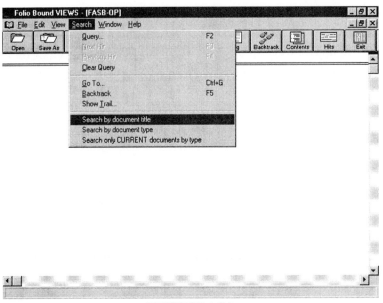

EXHIBIT 4-34

Click on "Search by document title." The query window shown in Exhibit 4-35 will appear:

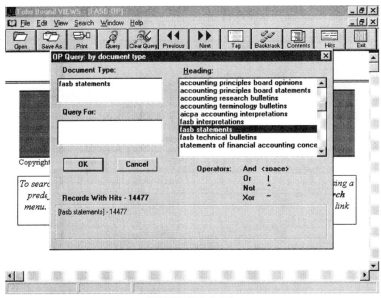

EXHIBIT 4-35

Using the mouse, move to the right-hand window marked "Heading" and click on the desired type of document. The desired document will appear in the upper left-hand window marked "Document Type." You must then type your query in the middle left-hand window "Query For." The results will show at the bottom of the query window.

When you click on the query box, the "Word" box will appear in the window on the right. The query, logic operators, word window, and results window are all activated as in any other search.

Searching by document title is a bit more challenging. First, using the Search pull-down menu, activate a search by document title. The document headings will appear in the window on the right. If you begin typing in a document number, the heading window will scroll down and highlight the document one space below from the typed request. For example, we typed "fas 1." The interface automatically added the single quotation mark in front of the request, and the heading window scrolled down automatically to fas 20 as shown in Exhibit 4-36.

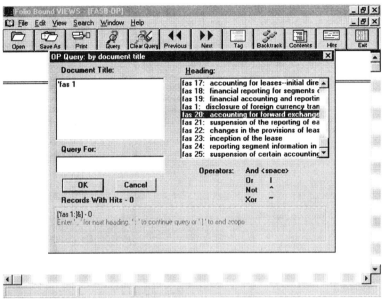

EXHIBIT 4-36

One important point to note is that the entire document title must appear in the Document Title window to begin this search. It is easier to cursor down to the appropriate pronouncement and double click on the pronouncement title, which will enter the document title in the "Document Title" window as shown in Exhibit 4-37.

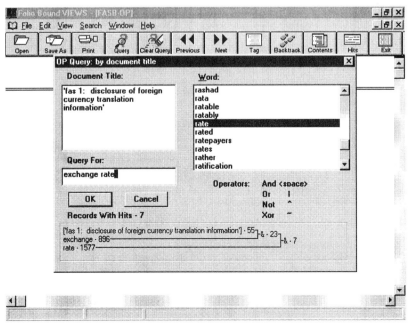

EXHIBIT 4-37

Notice the entire title was entered. You can then move your mouse to the Query For window and click once to activate the search. The word window will appear on the right-hand side, and the results window appears at the bottom. Again, the query window, word window, logic operators, and results are the same as our simple searches that we learned earlier in this course.

Searching by document title or document type is useful when you have already narrowed your search to specific areas of the infobase or specific standards. This type of search is used by individuals who are experienced accountants with a good research background, or by individuals who are familiar with the accounting standards.

Presenting Research Results

An effective researcher presents his or her results in a clear, concise manner. Your goal is to convince the other party (manager, client, attorney, tax authorities) that the position you have taken is appropriate for the given situation and that you have a reasonable basis of support or authority from the professional literature. Citing the appropriate authority gives your position its strength. This chapter has assisted you in developing the abilities to use electronic databases of authoritative literature. Upon mastering these skills, you are ready to begin applying them in the research process.

Exercise 4-34   Name: _____
Results & Table of Contents   Section: _____

You are interested in researching how to recognize interest expense on a zero coupon bond.

1.   Query *interest expense*. How many hits do you find?

      _____

2.   Click on contents. Read the accounting pronouncement topic headings. Which standards
      appear to be applicable?

      _____   _____

      _____   _____

      _____   _____

3.   Cursor down to the first standard you believe is applicable. Double click on this standard
      and read through this standard in sequential order. Indicate whether you believe this
      standard is on point and why.

      _____

      _____

      _____

4.   Using the View pull-down menu, view Records With Hits for your first applicable
      standard. Identify the cite of the first record in this standard with a hit.

      _____

5.   Return to the results of your query by using the Search pull-down menu. Click on Show
      Trail and cursor down to your query for *interest expense*. Double click on the query to
      retrieve the complete results of your search. Identify the first two
      cites from the text of results.

      _____   _____

Exercise 4-35   Name: _____

Results & Table of Contents   Section: _____

You are interested in researching how to recognize income for a franchise business.

1.   Query *franchise income*. How many hits do you find?

        _____

2.   Click on contents. Read the accounting pronouncement topic headings. Which standards appear to be applicable?

        _____   _____

        _____   _____

        _____   _____

3.   Cursor down to the first standard you believe is applicable. Double click on this standard and read through this standard in sequential order. Indicate whether you believe this standard is on point and why.

        _____

        _____

        _____

4.   Using the View pull-down menu, view Records With Hits for your first applicable standard. Identify the cite of the first record in this standard with a hit.

        _____

5.   Return to the results of your query by using the Search pull-down menu. Click on Show Trail and cursor down to your query for *franchise income*. Double click on the query to retrieve the complete results of your search. Identify the first two cites from the text of results.

        _____   _____

Exercise 4-36   **Name:** _____
Downloading and Printing   **Section:** _____

1.   Query for *accounts receivable*. How many hits do you find?

        _____

2.   Highlight ARB 43, Chapter 1A, Par. 5 and ARB 43, Chapter 3A, Par. 4 and copy them to
        the clipboard. Minimize FARS and move to a word processing program. Paste these two
        cites into a word processing document.

3.   Toggle back to FARS.   Highlight FAS 96, Par. 188 and copy it to the clipboard.
        Minimize FARS and place this in the word processing document with the previous two
        cites from No. 2. Print your results.

4.   Return to your query for *accounts receivable*. Access the full text of your results. Tag
        the following three records:

                ARB 43, Ch. 1A, Par. 5
                ARB 43, Ch. 3A, Par. 4
                FAS 96, Par. 188

        Save these three records as a word processing file. Retrieve this file using a
        word processing program. Print these three records.

5.   Examine the documents printed in No. 3 and No. 4 of this assignment. Explain any
        differences you see in the printed documents.

        _____

        _____

        _____

        _____

        _____

        _____

Exercise 4-37   Name: _____

Downloading and Printing   Section: _____

1.   Query for *mortgage backed securities*. How many hits do you find?

         _____

2.   Highlight FAS 65, Par. 4, FAS 65, Par. 5, and FAS 65, Par. 8, and copy them to the
         clipboard. Minimize FARS and move to a word processing program. Paste these three
         cites into a word processing document.

3.   Print your results from No. 2.

4.   Return to your query for *mortgage backed securities*. Access the full text of your results.
         Tag the following three records:

                 FAS 65, Par. 4
                 FAS 65, Par. 5
                 FAS 65, Par. 8

         Save these three records as a word processing file. Retrieve this file using a
         word processing program. Print these three records.

5.   Examine the documents printed in No. 3 and No. 4 of this assignment. Explain any
         differences you see in the printed documents.

_____

_____

_____

_____

_____

_____

Exercise 4-38   **Name:** _____

Critical Reading of the Literature   **Section:** _____

Develop at least three queries to search for answers to each of the following questions. Critically read the results to determine the best answer to each question. Download and print the appropriate citation to answer each question. Staple your downloaded answers to this page.

1.   What is inventory?

        Query #1   _____

        Query #2   _____

        Query #3   _____

        Additional
        Queries   _____

                               _____

2.   What is a financial instrument?

        Query #1   _____

        Query #2   _____

        Query #3   _____

        Additional
        Queries   _____

                               _____

Exercise 4-39   Name: _____
Critical Reading of the Literature   Section: _____

Develop at least three queries to search for answers to each of the following questions.
Critically read the results to determine the best answer to each question. Download and
print the appropriate citation to answer each question. Staple your downloaded answers to this
page.

1.   What is a contingency?

        Query #1   _____

        Query #2   _____

        Query #3   _____

        Additional
        Queries   _____

                         _____

2.   What are equity securities?

        Query #1   _____

        Query #2   _____

        Query #3   _____

        Additional
        Queries   _____

                         _____

Exercise 4-40   Name: _____

Advanced Search Commands   Section: _____

Develop keyword searches using advanced search commands with logic operators and nesting to solve each of the following cases. Write a research report indicating your recommendations for handling the case.

Great Buys sells computers. Suppose that early in 1998, Great Buys had 133 MHz computers remaining in its inventory at a time when customers were demanding faster computers. Great Buys paid $1,200 to its supplier for each of the machines. As of December 1998 Great Buys had 300 of these 133 MHz machines remaining in stock. As of December 1998, it is estimated that the 133 MHz machines are worth only $500 each. How should Great Buys handle the 133 MHz machines on its December 31, 1998, financial statements?

1.   Identify the issue in this case:

_____

_____

_____

2.   Develop search strings to research this case:

_____

_____

_____

_____

_____

_____

3.   Cite the appropriate literature that addresses this issue:

_____

_____

_____

4.   Explain how Great Buys should handle this situation on its 1998 financial statements.

_____

_____

_____

_____

_____

_____

_____

_____

_____

Exercise 4-41   Name: _____

Advanced Search Commands   Section: _____

Develop keyword searches using advanced search commands with logic operators and nesting to solve each of the following cases. Write a research report indicating your recommendations for handling the case.

Papierski Corporation has total assets of $3,000,000. The company has been named in a lawsuit for $1,200,000 that will go to trial in May 1999. While reviewing the case during the summer of 1998, the company's attorneys have concluded that Papierski is at fault and will most likely lose the suit. How should Papierski handle this issue on the December 31, 1998, financial statements?

1.   Identify the issue in this case:

_____

_____

_____

2.   Develop search strings to research this case:

_____

_____

_____

_____

_____

_____

3.   Cite the appropriate literature that addresses this issue:

_____

_____

_____

4.   Explain how Papierski should handle this situation on its 1998 financial statements.

_____

_____

_____

_____

_____

_____

_____

_____

_____

_____

_____

Chapter 5
The Applied Research Process

SUMMARY OF APPLIED RESEARCH PROCESS

The applied research process in accounting consists of several steps in an iterative process. Each step leads to the next, and the researcher may obtain additional information and insight during one step that may lead her back to a previous step for revision. Stressing that this general process is iterative is important. The competent researcher will move among steps and may actually complete some steps simultaneously. In addition, if no solution is realized from the process, the researcher may need to modify previous steps and repeat the process again. Following is a simple figure depicting the applied research process. We will describe and discuss each step later in this chapter. In addition, we provide an example of the applied research process using a financial reporting case to help you in understanding the process. Following is a diagram of the applied research process:

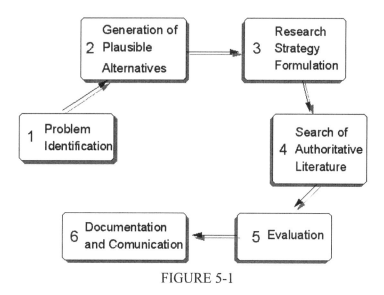

FIGURE 5-1

The applied research process consists of the following steps:
1. Problem identification and issue articulation, including the development of a problem statement;
2. Identification of plausible alternative solutions based upon prior knowledge or theory;
3. Generation of a research strategy, including keyword generation and choice of database or information resources;
4. Implementation of the research strategy through searching, identifying, and locating applicable information;
5. Analysis and evaluation of the information obtained, culminating in the development of a solution;
6. Documentation of the research process and communication of the research results.

To help in your understanding of this process, the following financial reporting case will be used to illustrate each step.

Gary Smith and Steve Jones started a pottery manufacturing business in 1968. Their company produces custom-designed flowerpots using a unique glazing process that results in very vibrant colors. Ever since its beginnings, Smith and Jones has focused on the artistic side of the business. The accounting system employed by Smith and Jones has also been quite simplistic. Inventory is valued at the costs of direct materials and direct labor, with all other costs and expenses accounted for as period expenses. Recently, the pottery produced by Smith and Jones has become quite popular and unmet demand has skyrocketed. To raise capital to expand its business, Smith and Jones is applying for a loan from the local bank. Given the amount it is asking to borrow, the bank has required Smith and Jones to provide financial statements prepared in conformance with generally accepted accounting principles. Your firm, Honest Abe Accountants, has been hired to assist in the preparation of the financial statements.

PROBLEM IDENTIFICATION

To correctly identify the accounting problem, it is important that you understand the transaction and/or the situation clearly. For a complex transaction, this may require you to draw a diagram of the transaction and depict the exchanges what will take place over time. Alternatively, or in addition, you may wish to consider the situation in terms of the basic accounting elements - assets, liabilities, equities, revenues, expenses, gains, and losses, both now and over time.

As previously discussed, most accounting problems requiring applied professional research are one or a combination of "what," "when," or "how" questions. In this case, the accounting issue involves the preparation of financial statements in conformance with generally accepted accounting principles and the appropriate measure of inventory cost. Accordingly, this issue has both "what" and "how" attributes. The issue is whether the company has correctly valued the inventory when it does not include overhead (indirect) costs. Accordingly, the issue involves a definition as well as measurement. Note that it is not the form of the question that causes its being both a "what" and a "how" question–it is the nature of the accounting issue itself.

By understanding the accounting elements involved in this situation, you, the researcher, can better determine the accounting problem. In this case, if inventory levels are remaining constant or growing, the omission of overhead costs from inventory results in a lower value on the inventory, lower total assets, lower cost of goods sold, lower net income due to higher operating expenses, and lower retained earnings than occur if overhead costs are included in inventory. If inventory levels are shrinking, higher net income occurs.

After identifying the accounting problem or issue, you should write a brief problem statement or question. This problem statement should succinctly summarize the accounting issue and should not be longer than one or two sentences. For the Smith and Jones case, the following problem statement is appropriate:

Is the exclusion of overhead costs from inventory in conformance with generally accepted accounting principles?

GENERATION OF PLAUSIBLE ALTERNATIVES

Given previous knowledge (both theoretical and practical), the researcher generates plausible alternatives for the identified problem statement. Often, this requires using your general accounting knowledge regarding the common accounting elements or measurement attributes. For the Smith and Jones case, the two most plausible alternatives are:

Yes, the exclusion of overhead costs from inventory is in conformance with generally accepted accounting principles.

No, the exclusion of overhead costs from inventory is *not* in conformance with generally accepted accounting principles.

These two alternatives become the basis for conducting the research. Similar to scientific research, applied professional research focuses on obtaining evidence (in this case, authoritative guidance from the professional pronouncements) to support or refute the alternatives.

After identifying the accounting issue or problem, writing out a problem statement, and developing plausible alternatives, you are ready to formulate a research strategy.

RESEARCH STRATEGY FORMULATION

Given the amount of information currently available to the professional accounting researcher, it is important the researcher formulates a strategy that will be employed in the search. This is key–it determines the extent of the search and provides a means for assessing the completion of the process. For example, the researcher must determine the types of information sources to be searched and develop keywords or phrases to be used. In addition, the researcher may specify the order in which she will gather the evidence for the different alternatives. *If* the researcher has strong priors that one of the alternatives is more likely to be correct, then a search that focuses on this most likely alternative first is most efficient. However, the researcher must still research the other alternatives if the evidence found supporting the first alternative does not negate the other alternatives.

For the Smith and Jones case, the problem statement helps in formulating the strategy. Since the issue concerns compliance with generally accepted accounting principles, the focus of your search for supporting or negating the plausible alternatives is on the authoritative literature regarding generally accepted accounting principles. This means that the target pronouncements are those of the Financial Accounting Standards Board and its predecessors. In this case, the professional literature regarding auditing or tax is not applicable.

An essential element of conducting applied research, particularly with electronic databases, is the generation of keywords or key phrases on which to conduct the research. This component of the process should link directly to the problem statement and the keywords or phrases (or synonyms for them) should be embedded in the problem statement. A direct link between the problem statement and the keywords to be used must exist. A thesaurus may be helpful in generating synonyms. Additional assistance may be found by appealing to the indices at the end of textbooks in which the general topic of the case is discussed.

Recall the problem statement generated for the Smith and Jones case:

Is the exclusion of overhead costs from inventory in conformance with generally accepted accounting principles?

A number of keywords are apparent in this problem statement–*overhead*, *costs*, *inventory*, and *exclusion*. Usually, words that are less general and more specific will target the search better–*overhead*, *inventory*, and *exclusion.* *Cost* is excluded since it is a much more general term and lacks the precision of the other three.

Since the researcher may not be using the same terminology as that used in the pronouncements, identifying several synonyms for the keywords above is important. Following are several alternative words that might be useful in conducting the research.

overhead	inventory	exclusion
fixed costs	goods	omission
fixed overhead	raw materials	elimination
indirect costs	work in process	
indirect labor	finished goods	
indirect materials		

Besides generating synonyms, considering alternative forms of the words is also important. For example,

> overhead–overheads;
> inventory–inventories–inventoried–inventoriable;
> exclusion–exclusions–excluded–exclude–excludes.

Since the search engines for most electronic professional accounting literature databases contain wildcards, using a wildcard approach that allows searching across various forms of the terms is usually appropriate and ensures that the search is comprehensive.

At this point, a problem statement has been identified, plausible alternatives have been generated, and a research strategy, including both the sources to be searched and the keywords to employ, has been formulated for the Smith and Jones case. Conducting the search of the authoritative literature is now appropriate.

SEARCH OF THE AUTHORITATIVE LITERATURE

The goal of the search of the authoritative literature is to provide evidence that will support or negate the plausible alternatives that we have identified. Accordingly, an exhaustive search of the applicable literature is required. The professional literature database chosen to be researched is the Financial Accounting Research System (FARS), as shown in Exhibit 5-1.

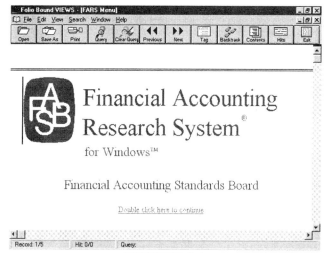

EXHIBIT 5-1

Since adequate documentation of the solution requires the specific citations used as evidence to support or negate the alternatives, this search will focus on the original pronouncements, Exhibit 5-2, as the primary target.

Since it is not known whether this is a topic recently considered by the authoritative standard setters, a complete search of all sources, both recent and old, is appropriate. In cases in which you know the topic is recent or current, you may wish to limit your search only to recent pronouncements.

Original Pronouncement Sections

◊ Committee on Accounting Procedure Accounting Research Bulletins (ARB)

◊ Accounting Principles Board Opinions (APB)

◊ AICPA Accounting Interpretations (AIN)

◊ Accounting Principles Board Statements (APS)

◊ Accounting Terminology Bulletins (ATB)

Financial Accounting Standards Board:

◊ Statements of Financial Accounting Standards (FAS)
◊ Interpretations (FIN)
◊ Technical Bulletins (FTB)
◊ Statements of of Financial Accounting Concepts (CON)

EXHIBIT 5-2

The search to be conducted focuses on the three terms identified previously–*inventory*, *overhead*, and *exclusion*. Since various forms of these words could be appropriate, the search is conducted using "wildcards"–*inventor**; *overhead**; and *exclu**.

As shown in this screen (Exhibit 5-3), there are three authoritative literature passages (hits) that need to be examined.

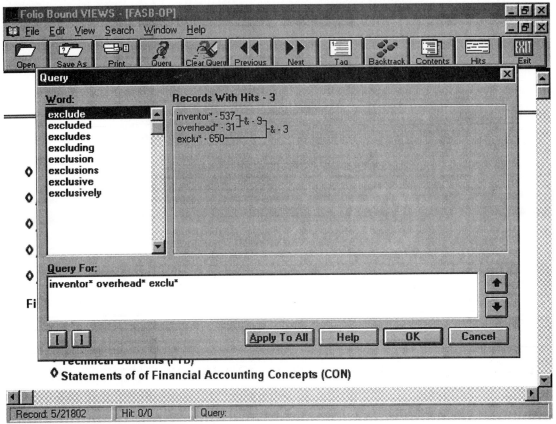

EXHIBIT 5-3

EVALUATION OF SEARCH RESULTS

The evaluation of the search results must consider two attributes. First, it must be determined if the literature found is directly applicable or if it is applicable by analogy. If the passage is directly on-point, then the conclusion may be easy to make. However, if the passage is only applicable through analogy, then the researcher must examine the extent to which the facts of the case and the problem statement correspond to the situation being addressed in the professional pronouncement. Second, considering the level of authority for the pronouncement in which the applicable passage is found is important.

For the Smith and Jones case, the three "hits" need to be read and analyzed. A brief skimming of the first hit, Accounting Research Bulletin 43, Chapter 4, paragraph 5 (provided in Exhibit 5-4), indicates that this passage may be germane to the issue here. This passage is discussing the propriety of accounting for inventory at cost and defines the nature of those costs. In particular, the passage explicitly states that the exclusion of overhead costs for inventory is not generally accepted accounting.

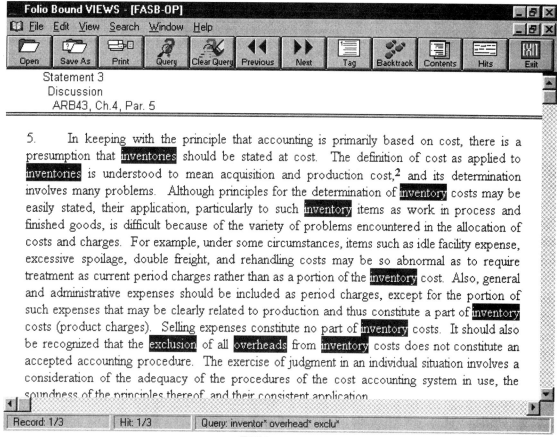

EXHIBIT 5-4

Although you might conclude that the search is over, evaluating the other passages is important. Some inconsistencies exist between the professional pronouncements and the search must be exhaustive. The other hits might provide additional support or they might contradict this passage.

The second hit, shown in Exhibit 5-5, is FIN 1, paragraph 2. This is a Financial Accounting Standards Board Interpretation. The third hit, also displayed in Exhibit 5-5, is from SFAC 2, paragraph 6–a Statement of Financial Accounting Concepts provided by the Financial Accounting Standards Board. A quick scan of these hits shows that both address the issue and are consistent with the first passage. Accordingly, although these hits are considered lower-level GAAP (lower level in the authoritative hierarchy), they do provide additional support.

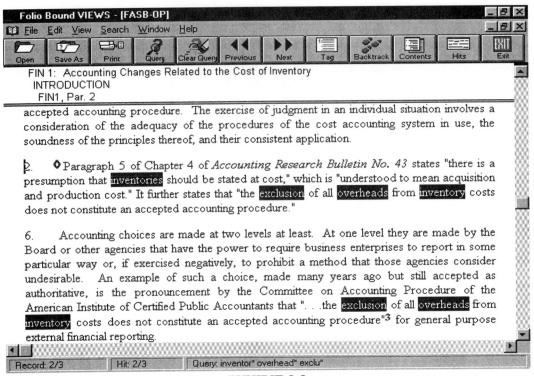

EXHIBIT 5-5

Recall, that the two plausible alternatives are the following:

Yes, the exclusion of overhead costs from inventory is in conformance with generally accepted accounting principles.

No, the exclusion of overhead costs from inventory is *not* in conformance with generally accepted accounting principles.

The three hits or cites provide direct support for the second alternative and directly negate the first alternative. Based upon these results, the conclusion is that the method of accounting currently employed by Smith and Jones does not constitute generally accepted accounting principles.

DOCUMENTING THE RESULTS AND COMMUNICATING YOUR SOLUTION

Documenting the applied research process and the results, as well as communicating the solution, is as important as conducting a comprehensive search and determining a correct solution. The applied research process culminates, and its success ultimately depends upon adequate documentation and communication. That documentation usually includes a research file memorandum for establishing a file or record of the research. In addition, a communication memorandum is prepared for transmittal of the results.

Both the file documentation and the communication memorandum must be concise and grammatically correct. Persons scrutinizing your documentation may form judgments about the quality of the research you conducted and judgments of your qualifications as a researcher. These judgments may be based upon the clarity and appearance of the written documents. Both the file memorandum and the communication memorandum also may assist you when communicating the results of the research orally.

Adequate documentation is essential for depicting the research process that has been accomplished. It is also important that adequate documentation be prepared so that others may use the research results in the future. In addition, adequate documentation provides a record for you when you are called upon a few years in the future to defend your solution.

Since applied professional research in accounting is usually focused on resolution of a problem, it is important to be able to communicate the answer succinctly. Use short sentences with unambiguous words and terminology. The objective is maximum clarity and the portrayal of professional competence and objectivity.

Both the communication memorandum and the file memorandum should be written in an analytical style. Although the format may vary, these documents should contain the following:

1. A brief summary of the relevant facts and the situation surrounding the issue of interest.
2. A statement of the research problem.
3. A description of the plausible alternatives.
4. A summary of the proposed solution.
5. A documentation of the authoritative support on which the solution is based.

The research file memorandum is usually more detailed and may also contain references to the keywords searched as well as assumptions made.

The fact summary is important since it sets the stage for the analysis and conclusions. A concise description of the situation in which the problem or issue underlying the applied research needs to be provided. We should also include any assumptions regarding the situation as well as other pertinent information for understanding the context in which the problem occurs.

The problem statement must clearly identify the specific questions or issues to be answered. The problem statement should only be brief. Typically, the problem statement prepared at the beginning of the applied research process can be used to define the problem in your documentation. Since keywords are essential to the applied research process, framing the issue(s) incorrectly in the problem statement may cause one to overlook important aspects of the situation or address the wrong issue.

All alternatives considered should be explicitly described. Any theoretical or practical justification for any of the alternatives should also be mentioned.

The proposed solution summary should be brief and to the point. It should not include caveats, unless they are part of the actual situation. In addition, conclusions for each of the problem statements or questions are needed. The conclusion should allow the reader to understand the reasoning for the proposed solution without having to read the authoritative literature. The proposed solutions should be clear and concise and any qualifications or contingencies must be stated.

The evidence or documentation should be the most detailed and should summarize both the researcher's reasoning as well as the authoritative support. References to the applicable authoritative literature supporting and refuting the plausible alternatives are appropriate, although the focus should be on the authoritative literature underlying the proposed solution. The alternatives may be briefly discussed and evidence demonstrating their disqualification should be provided. Appropriately cite the authoritative literature used in the solution but use quotes sparingly.

On the following pages are examples of a research file memorandum and a communication memorandum (client letter) for the Smith and Jones case. Note that the research file memorandum and the communication memorandum contain a great deal of overlap. However, the research file memorandum is more complete and provides better documentation of the research process. The client letter is less technical and focuses on explaining the solution in lay terms.

Upon completion of these two memoranda, this applied research inquiry is finished. An exhaustive authoritative literature search has produced a solution and the results have been adequately documented and communicated.

To make sure you understand this process, you may wish to conduct the process on your own, using this illustration as an example. Developing the skills of applied research are best learned by experience–practice, practice, and more practice!!

Research File Memorandum

June 24, 1997

Research File Memorandum

Prepared by David A. Ziebart

Client: Smith and Jones

Subject: propriety of excluding overhead costs from inventory

Background: Smith and Jones, a privately held entity, is being required to submit financial statements prepared in conformance with generally accepted accounting principles as part of a loan application at the local bank. Only direct labor and direct material costs have been included in the inventory cost valuation. Previously, all overhead costs have been treated as period expenses. It is assumed that the magnitude of these costs are material.

Statement of research problem or question: Is the exclusion of overhead effs from inventory in conformance with generally accepted accounting principles?

Plausible alternatives: The plausible alternatives range from including all overhead costs in inventory to including no overhead costs in inventory. Between these two extremes would be positions in which some portion of overhead costs would be included.

Proposed solution: The exclusion of overhead costs from inventory is not in conformance with generally accepted accounting principles. Accordingly, overhead costs should be capitalized as a component of inventory and should not be treated as a period expense.

Explanation and documentation: The research underlying this solution was conducted using the Financial Accounting Research System (FARS). The version of FARS used was current through January 15, 1997. The Original Pronouncements database as well as the Emerging Issues Task Force database were searched for applicable guidance. The keywords used were *overhead**, *inventor**, and *exclu**. This resulted in three sources of guidance that apply to the research issue–ARB 43, Ch. 4, Par. 5; FIN 1, Par. 2; and SFAC 2, Par. 6. These sources are consistent in requiring the inclusion of overhead costs in inventory and directly address the issue.

Other issues and additional considerations: Since the exclusion of overhead from inventory is not in conformance with generally accepted accounting principles, the previous year's financial statements of Smith and Jones are also not in conformance with GAAP. If called upon to audit the statements, there will need to be a change in the accounting method and there may be additional documentation and research for a change from an unacceptable method to one that is acceptable.

Communication Memorandum (client letter)

June 24, 1997

Smith and Jones
414 East 4th Street
Champaign, Illinois 76543

Dear Gary and Steve:

Per your request to assist you in preparing your company's financial statements
in conformance with generally accepted accounting principles, I have determined
that your current practice of excluding overhead costs from inventory is not
appropriate.

It is my understanding that the local bank requires a set of financial statements
prepared in conformance with generally accepted accounting principles as part of
your loan application. In order to comply, overhead costs will need to be
included in inventory and cost of goods sold for current period's statement of
financial position and statement of earnings. Since statements of previous
periods were not prepared in conformance with generally accepted accounting
principles, adjustments will need to be made if they are to be included with the
current period's statements.

The basis for my conclusion is the result of a search of the authoritative literature
that constitutes generally accepted accounting principles. That literature directly
addresses the issue and requires overhead costs related to the production of
inventory be included as a cost of inventory and cost of goods sold (when sold).

Should you need additional information or clarification, please contact me. I
would certainly welcome the opportunity to discuss this issue with you.

Sincerely,

David A. Ziebart

Exercise 5-1   Name: _____

Applying the Research Steps   Section: _____

Instructions: Using the following case information, complete the worksheet questions below.

Zackie Company has recently allowed its customers to make purchases on credit. The terms are 2/10, n/30. Unfortunately, Zackie Company has found that not all of its credit customers pays their bill on time. Accordingly, Zackie Company has estimated an allowance for uncollectible accounts and will match this bad debt expense against the credit sales. On Zackie Company's financial statements, the allowance for uncollectible accounts is classified as a current liability.

Part 1. What is the potential accounting problem?

_____

_____

_____

_____

Part 2. Prepare a problem statement or question on which you would conduct applied professional research.

_____

_____

_____

_____

Part 3. Identify two plausible alternative solutions for the accounting issue you identified above.

1. _____

_____

_____

2. _____

_____

_____

Part 4. Generate a list of keywords or key phrases you would use to research this issue.

_____   _____

_____   _____

_____   _____

Part 5. Search the FARS Original Pronouncements database using the keywords, and identify the passages that are applicable to this problem. If you do not find any passages that are applicable, generate a new set of keywords or key phrases and try again.

Cite: _____   Cite: _____

Cite: _____   Cite: _____

Cite: _____   Cite: _____

Cite: _____   Cite: _____

Part 6. Prepare a communication memorandum and a file memorandum documenting your proposed solution for this situation. Be sure to use good form and check both spelling and grammar.

Exercise 5-2   **Name:** _____

Applying the Research Steps   **Section:**_____

Instructions: Using the following case information, complete the worksheet questions below.

> Good Deals sells electronic equipment and household appliances. In order to
> improve employee morale, the company made an employee lounge that will
> contain a nicely equipped lunchroom. Equipment in the lounge includes two
> microwaves, a large screen television, a VCR, a fully equipped computer, a
> refrigerator, and a stove. As a means of familiarizing the employees (especially
> the sales staff) with the features of new products, new equipment is taken from
> the showroom floor and placed in the lounge every few months. The old
> equipment is returned to the showroom floor and sold as demonstration units.
> On January 3, 1997, the manager of the store placed the first equipment in the
> lounge. On December 15, 1997, all of the original equipment was taken back to
> the showroom floor and new equipment was brought to the lounge.

Part 1. What is the potential accounting problem?

_____

_____

_____

_____

Part 2. Prepare a problem statement or question on which you would conduct applied
professional research.

_____

_____

_____

_____

Part 3. Identify two plausible alternative solutions for the accounting issue you identified.

1 _____

_____

_____

2 _____

_____

_____

Part 4. Generate a list of keywords or key phrases you would use to research this issue.

_____   _____

_____   _____

_____   _____

Part 5. Search the FARS Original Pronouncements database using the keywords and identify the passages that are applicable to this problem. If you do not find any passages that are applicable, generate a new set of keywords or key phrases and try again.

Cite: _____   Cite: _____

Cite: _____   Cite: _____

Cite: _____   Cite: _____

Cite: _____   Cite: _____

Part 6. Prepare a communication memorandum and a file memorandum documenting your proposed solution for this situation. Be sure to use good form and check both spelling and grammar.

Exercise 5-3   **Name:** _____

Applying the Research Steps   **Section:** _____

Instructions: Using the following case information, complete the worksheet questions below.

> Ribbitt is a small company that operates in Florida by marketing grow-a-frog kits to large toy stores and discount retailers. Each grow-a-frog kit contains a small plastic aquarium tank, gravel, a plastic plant, and a coupon redeemable for one live tadpole. A large inventory of tadpoles are kept on hand at all times. To ensure a ready supply of tadpoles, one thousand adult frogs are kept on hand. The reproductive life of an adult frog is about nine months. At that time, the frogs are harvested and sold to J. Lafitte's Fine Froglegs. Both the adult frogs and the tadpoles were classified as inventory on Ribbitt's financial statements. Recently, through selective breeding, the reproductive life of the adult frogs has been extended to three years.

Part 1. What is the potential accounting problem?

_____

_____

_____

_____

Part 2. Prepare a problem statement or question on which you would conduct applied professional research.

_____

_____

_____

_____

Part 3. Identify two plausible alternative solutions for the accounting issue you identified.

1_____

_____

_____

2_____

_____

_____

Part 4. Generate a list of keywords or key phrases you would use to research this issue.

_____   _____

_____   _____

_____   _____

Part 5. Search the FARS Original Pronouncements database using the keywords, and identify the passages that are applicable to this problem. If you do not find any passages that are applicable, generate a new set of keywords or key phrases and try again.

Cite: _____   Cite: _____

Cite: _____   Cite: _____

Cite: _____   Cite: _____

Cite: _____   Cite: _____

Part 6. Prepare a communication memorandum and a file memorandum documenting your proposed solution for this situation. Be sure to use good form and check both spelling and grammar.

Chapter 6
Understanding Complex
Transactions and Problems

IDENTIFYING AND UNDERSTANDING COMPLEX PROBLEMS AND ISSUES

Typically, the problem or issue of interest may be very complex and involve multiple parties or entities. Understanding the transaction or issue completely to research a solution adequately is important for the researcher. Failure to understand the problem or transaction may result in the misidentification of the problem. This may lead to an incorrect problem statement and the research conducted will be flawed.

It is essential that you, the researcher, understand the transaction or issue and be able to describe and explain it. If you are unable to explain it to another person, you probably do not adequately understand it yourself.

When trying to understand a complex transaction or issue or when trying to explain it to another person, a diagram or multiple diagrams may help. This may involve the preparation of a simple chart using stick figures combined with arrows and lines or a more sophisticated flowchart depicting various components of the transaction. A graphical representation may consist of a chart that shows the relationships among various parties to a transaction or the preparation of a time line that shows the timing of various events germane to the issue or transaction of importance.

A simple transaction or situation may require only a simple chart. For example, consider the following financial reporting issue.

> Luce Bruce Company (the lessor) has entered a leasing arrangement with D-Mar Brothers (the lessee). The leased asset has a fair market value of $100,000 and cost Luce Bruce Company $93,000. It has structured the lease so that D-Mar Brothers will pay five annual payments of $15,000, and D-Mar Brothers guarantees the residual value of the asset to be $30,000 at the end of the five-year lease. D-Mar Brothers has taken out an insurance policy with Insure-U Cheap that will make up any difference between the fair market value of the asset and $30,000. The cost of the insurance policy is $4,000, payable at the beginning of the lease.

A simple graphical representation or diagram may help in understanding or explaining this situation. Figure 6-1 is an example of such a diagram.

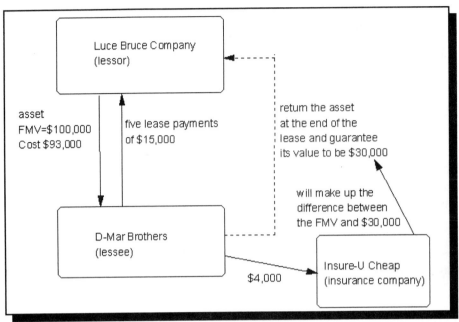

FIGURE 6-1

Note that the diagram does not have to be artistic. Instead, functionality is key–the diagram captures the main aspects of the situation and graphically depicts the cash flows involved.

An illustration of a more complex agreement requiring several diagrams follow:

Kaag & Kaag, an oil exploration company, has entered several joint agreements in which it leases the mineral rights on parcels of land it plans to explore. As part of the mineral rights agreements, Kaag & Kaag has entered into a contract with J.W. Kaag, Inc., a separate entity. J.W. Kaag, Inc. manages mineral rights for various entities and individuals. In return for managing the mineral rights, J.W. Kaag, Inc. collects a monthly fee of $10 per acre from the owner of the land, to a maximum of $120 per acre. The contract calls for Kaag & Kaag to obtain the rights to mine any minerals found, and in return, to guarantee a certain amount (usually $5,000), to be paid to the landowner if valuable minerals are found. This guaranteed amount, termed the residual, will be paid when production occurs or it sells production rights to another party. Once production commences, Kaag & Kaag, J.W. Kaag, Inc., and the owner of the property will share equally in the proceeds from the sale of the minerals. Kaag & Kaag bears all costs of production. If the production rights are sold to another party, Kaag & Kaag, J.W. Kaag, Inc., and the landowner will share equally in the proceeds. If the proceeds from the sale of the production rights are less than the guaranteed residual, both Kaag & Kaag and J.W. Kaag, Inc. are equally responsible for the difference. If no minerals are found, Kaag & Kaag will reimburse J.W. Kaag for any legal or related fees associated with managing the land parcel. If minerals are found and mined, Kaag & Kaag is not responsible for reimbursement of legal or related fees and J.W. Kaag, Inc. will bear the full cost. Kaag & Kaag bears all land reclamation costs but J.W. Kaag, Inc. guarantee the reclamation to the owner's satisfaction.

Figure 6-2 is a tree diagram representing the significant events in the agreement.

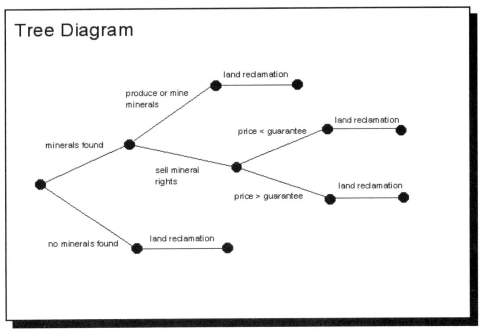

FIGURE 6-2

To more completely represent the various aspects of this transaction, we produce the following set of diagrams depicting the major events. A representation of the three initial parties in this situation result in the following diagram (Figure 6-3).

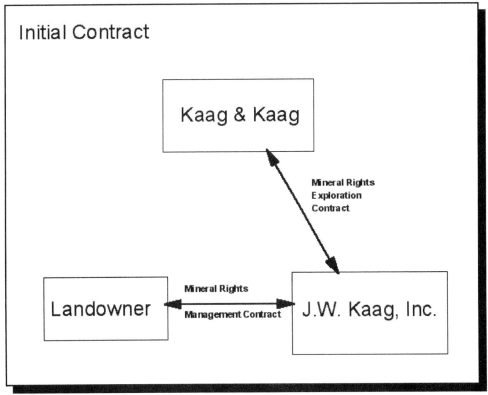

FIGURE 6-3

Depicting the management fee paid to J.W. Kaag, Inc. by the owner further enhances the diagram in Figure 6-4.

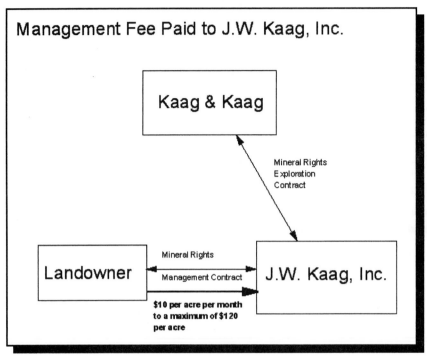

FIGURE 6-4

Adding the payment of the residual value further illustrates the situation and the cash flows that will occur if a significant amount of minerals is discovered. Figure 6-5 illustrates this aspect.

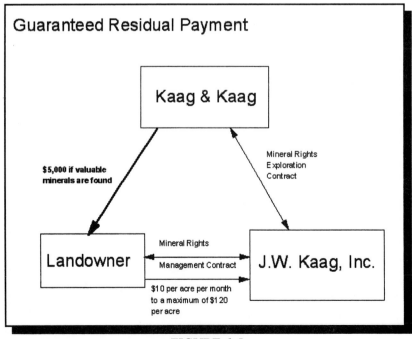

FIGURE 6-5

If minerals are found, and Kaag & Kaag mines the minerals and sells them, and the revenue from the sale of the minerals is split evenly between Kaag & Kaag, J.W. Kaag, Inc., and the landowner. The diagram titled "Sale of Mined Minerals" (Figure 6-6) depicts this scenario.

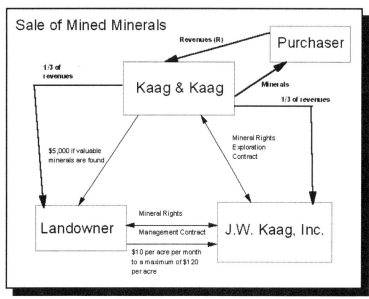

FIGURE 6-6

Alternatively, after finding a significant deposit of minerals, Kaag & Kaag could sell the rights to the minerals to another entity that would actually mine them and then sell them. If this occurs, two alternatives become important. If the selling price is less than the guaranteed residual amount, Kaag & Kaag and J.W. Kaag, Inc. will make up the difference between the sales price and the guaranteed residual. Figure 6-7 illustrates this scenario. However, if the selling price is greater than the guaranteed residual, it is split equally between Kaag & Kaag, J.W. Kaag, Inc., and the landowner. This is illustrated in Figure 6-8.

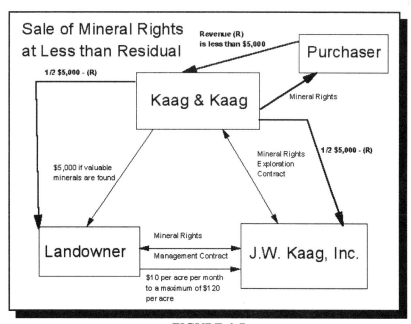

FIGURE 6-7

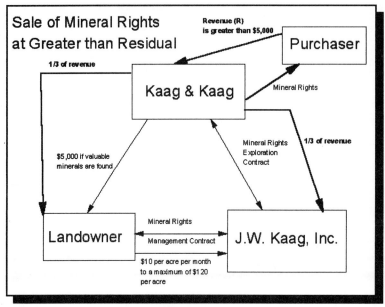

FIGURE 6-8

Upon completion of the mining activities, Kaag & Kaag is responsible for the land reclamation activities, while J.W. Kaag, Inc. has guaranteed the reclamation will meet the approval of the landowner. Figure 6-9 attempts to show this relationship.

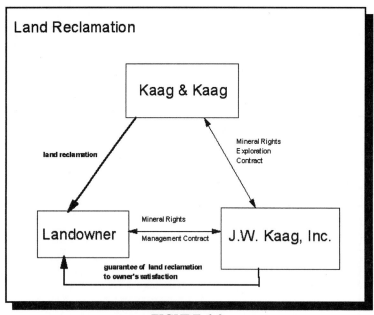

FIGURE 6-9

If no significant minerals are found, Kaag & Kaag is responsible for reimbursing J.W. Kaag, Inc. for any legal or related costs associated with the exploration activities on the land. We depict this in Figure 6-10.

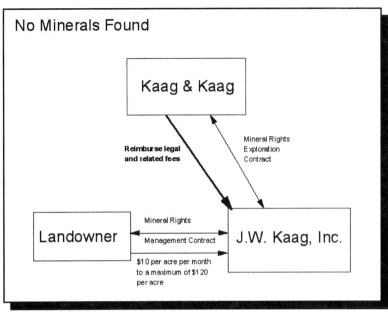

FIGURE 6-10

As you can see, this series of diagrams reflects several aspects of this transaction and reflects alternative scenarios. Such a series may enhance your understanding of the issues and make it easier to communicate your understanding. Elaborate artwork is not needed and it is the process of preparing the diagrams that usually clarifies your understanding. Also, different individuals may have very different perspectives on how to represent the situation.

Various media can be used to illustrate complex transactions and situations in accounting. Simple stick people diagrams may be useful, or flowcharts and graphical techniques can be used to illustrate the situation or transaction. The representations can be done freehand, with templates, or using graphical computer software. Using computer presentation software, we can construct more sophisticated representations with sound effects, moving images, and video and audio clips. The essential element is to be able to communicate the transaction or situation. This requires that you understand it and can depict your understanding. Sophisticated graphics are not a good substitute for a solid understanding of the situation. In addition, simplicity of the illustration(s) may help others' comprehension.

Notes:

Exercise 6-1 Name: _____

Illustrating a Simple Scenario Section: _____

Instructions: Prepare a diagram of the following situation using your own perspective and tools. Do not replicate the diagram illustrated in this chapter. Instead, use your own ideas.

Queens Company (the lessor) has entered a leasing arrangement with Smith Construction (the lessee). The leased asset has a fair market value of $1,000,000 and cost Queens Company $983,000. The lease is structured so that Smith Construction will pay five annual payments of $150,000. In addition, Smith Construction is required to pay $1,000 per month in maintenance fees to Queens Company. Smith Construction guarantees the residual value of the asset to be $300,000 at the end of the five-year lease. Smith Construction is required to carry insurance on the equipment at a cost of $4,000 per year. Proof of insurance is required at the beginning of each year.

Trade diagrams with a classmate. *Classmate's name:_____*

Without looking at the described scenario above, use the diagram prepared by your classmate and prepare a brief paragraph describing what the diagram depicts to you.

_____

_____

_____

_____

_____

Does the diagram adequately depict the transaction? _____

If not, why not? What is missing? _____

_____

_____

Exercise 6-2   Name: _____

Illustrating a Complex Transaction   Section: _____

Instructions: Prepare a diagram of the following situation using your own perspective and tools. Be creative!

To guarantee a steady stream of raw materials for production at a relatively fixed price, Davis Enterprises persuaded BobLink Materials to build a production facility next to Davis Enterprises' factory. Davis Enterprises produces wet suits for use in marine recreation. Davis Enterprises manufactures sheets of neoprene rubber which are used to make the wet suits. To entice BobLink to build its plant, Davis Enterprises leases the land on which the factory is to be built to BobLink for a period of 100 years at a cost of $1.00 per year. The land has a fair market value of $1,200,000, and the fair market value of the lease payments would be $20,000 per year. Davis Enterprises guarantees to purchase 400,000 square yards of neoprene fabric per year on a direct cost plus basis. The price paid by Davis Enterprises will cover all direct costs of production plus twenty percent. BobLink will bill Davis Enterprises monthly for the past month's production and Davis Enterprises has the right to contest the bill for three months. It will resolve any contest to the bill via an independent arbitration board containing three independent lawyers.

Trade diagrams with a classmate.   *Classmate's name:* _____

Without looking at the described scenario above, use the diagram prepared by your classmate and prepare a brief paragraph describing what the diagram depicts to you.

_____

_____

_____

_____

_____

Does the diagram adequately depict the transaction? _____

If not, why not? What is missing? _____

_____

_____

Exercise 6-3   Name: _____

Illustrating a Complex Transaction   Section: _____

Instructions: Prepare a diagram of the following situation using your own perspective and tools. Be creative!

Selby's Automart, a local automobile dealership, sells extended warranties to many of its customers. Third-party companies offer the extended warranties and extend the original auto manufacturer's warranty. The purchaser of the warranty may choose the length of time for the extension and pays accordingly. Most customers choose to extend the warranty to six years or 100,000 miles, whichever occurs first. The typical cost of the extended warranty is about $1,000. Selby's profit on the sale of a typical extended warranty is about $300. As an added incentive for customers to purchase the warranty, Selby's gives the purchasers a book of fifty $20 coupons. Each coupon can only be used during a particular period or mileage. For instance, the first coupon can be used during the first four months of ownership or between zero and 3,000 miles. Coupons can be used for typical services and maintenance and also any major repairs. Once the time or mileage has expired, the coupon may not be used. For services less than the $20 face amount of the coupon, no actual cash is involved and the customer does not get a refund for the difference.

Trade diagrams with a classmate.   ***Classmate's name:_____***

Without looking at the described scenario above, use the diagram prepared by your classmate and prepare a brief paragraph describing what the diagram depicts to you.

_____

_____

_____

_____

Does the diagram adequately depict the transaction? _____

If not, why not? What is missing? _____

_____

_____

Exercise 6-4   Name: _____

Illustrating a Complex Transaction   Section: _____

Instructions: Prepare a diagram of the following situation using your own perspective and tools. Be creative!

Jones Trucking, in Atlanta, Georgia, owns a large warehouse facility in Moab, Utah. Unfortunately, due to changes in routes and a restructuring of its customer base, it significantly underutilizes the warehouse in Moab. Western Shipping, a transportation services company, owns a large warehouse near Washington, D.C., which has been closed for three years. Jones Trucking has been looking to acquire a warehouse in the Baltimore-D.C. area while Western Shipping needs some warehouse capabilities in eastern Utah or western Colorado. Rather than selling their warehouses, Jones Trucking and Western Shipping have entered an agreement to swap the use of their vacant warehouses. Both entities will continue to own their warehouses and will be responsible for all maintenance and repairs. However, each will make its warehouse facility available to the other on a per-use basis. The negotiated storage fee will be $.01 per pound per twenty-four-hour period. Since neither entity knows exactly how much storage it will use, each entity will keep track of the other's use and will settle at the end of each month. However, the maximum charge for any month will be limited to the current rental rate for a similar capacity facility. In addition, the agreement also contains a clause allowing payment to be in the form of transportation and shipping services, if both parties agree. This agreement has an initial term of two years but can be canceled upon sixty days' written notice by either party.

Trade diagrams with a classmate.   *Classmate's name:* _____

Without looking at the described scenario above, use the diagram prepared by your classmate and prepare a brief paragraph describing what the diagram depicts to you.

_____

_____

_____

_____

_____

Does the diagram adequately depict the transaction? _____

If not, why not? What is missing? _____

_____

_____

Chapter 7
Applied Research
in Tax Accounting

OVERVIEW

Tax research is similar to financial accounting research. Both require identification of the issues involved, review of the relevant literature and/or authoritative sources, and the formulation of a solution. This chapter builds on the material in the previous chapters and assumes that the reader is familiar with the use of electronic infobases and the Internet. It presents the three primary tax sources and their locations. Then, we discuss the tax research methodology using keywords. A sample research case concludes the chapter.

TAX AND FINANCIAL REPORTING OBJECTIVES

Although the research methodology is similar, there are fundamental differences between the reporting objectives of financial and tax accounting. Fiscal and social policies form the bases for the tax laws. The need to generate a certain level of revenue or to encourage certain social behavior may result in reporting requirements that are different from those for financial reporting purposes. Additionally, the overriding fiscal or social concerns change from one period to the next, resulting in different (and sometimes opposite) tax consequences from one year to the next for the same transaction. This has been especially true for the last twenty years in which the federal government has passed numerous major pieces of legislation that have either added, deleted, or modified the laws governing federal income taxes. The laws and interpretations thereof encompass thousands of pages of statutes, regulations, court decisions, and other administrative interpretations of the intent and requirements of the laws.

On the other hand, the essence of financial reporting is to break down a transaction to identify the economic substance of what has transpired. Once this has been done, reporting issues focus on the appropriate way in which to disclose this transaction's substance to the user of the financial statement. The objective is to provide information that is useful for meeting the needs of the investor. Thus, for financial reporting purposes, the researcher is focusing upon the substance of the transaction rather than the form of the transaction.

An example of the substance over form approach in financial accounting is the requirement to capitalize certain financing leases when they meet specific criteria. Capitalization is required when the substance of the transaction is deemed to be a financing arrangement. Although the parties to the transaction may have legally enforceable documents that label the transaction as a lease, it is still reported for financial purposes as the purchase of an asset along with the corresponding recording of liabilities and depreciation of the capitalized costs in future reporting periods. Thus, the substance of the transaction takes precedence over the form for financial reporting purposes.

In contrast to this, the ultimate user of information reported for tax purposes is the taxing authority. The taxing authority is interested in the correct determination of the amount of taxes to be paid as the result of the transaction. Because tax laws are founded in fiscal and social policy, two transactions that have the same economic substance but different forms can result in two different tax consequences. In the next section, the substance versus form issue is illustrated by comparing the tax treatment of transactions involving a tax-exempt entity and a taxable entity.

Substance versus Form

Certain entities are granted exemption from federal income taxes due to the social function they serve. These include charitable organizations, schools, hospitals, and other organizations that perform functions the government deems to be socially desirable. Furthermore, in order to encourage public support of these organizations, donations made to these entities may be deductible in determining the taxable income of a taxable corporation. The following two examples illustrate how the **form** of the donation affects the tax consequences.

Big Time Bucks Corporation (a taxable corporation), in administering its corporate good citizenship policies, wishes to donate $20,000 to the local branch of the American Heart Fund (a qualifying charitable organization). Big Time owns stock of a publicly traded company that it purchased several years ago. The stock cost Big Time $5,000 and has a current value of $20,000. Big Time sells the stock and then donates the $20,000 cash proceeds from the sale to the charity. The result of these two transactions is the reporting for tax purposes of a $15,000 gain on the sale of the stock ($20,000 proceeds less $5,000 cost) and the $20,000 deduction for the cash donation. The net effect is a $5,000 decrease in Big Time's corporate taxable income.

Consider the same facts as in the preceding example, except instead of selling the stock, Big Time gives the stock to the Heart Fund and the charity then sells the stock to get the $20,000 cash it needs. The donation by Big Time results in a $20,000 reduction of Big Time taxable income (fair market value of the stock donated). Since the Heart Fund is a qualifying charity, neither the receipt of the stock nor the subsequent gain on the sale of the stock is taxable to the Heart Fund.

The economic substance of the two transactions described above is identical yet their tax consequences are different. The only difference in the form of the transaction is who sold the stock. When the dust has settled, Big Time no longer has an asset worth $20,000 and the Heart Fund has $20,000 of cash to use for its operations. In the first example, Big Time has only reduced its taxable income by $5,000 as opposed to the situation in the second example where its taxable income has been reduced by $20,000.

These two examples provide an illustration of how the form of a transaction overrides the substance of the transaction due to the influence of social policy upon the governing statutes. The statutes allow the deduction of the fair market value of the stock in order to encourage taxpayers to support worthy organizations. Additionally, the statutes do not tax the charitable organization on its receipt of such stock or its subsequent sale. These laws were originally enacted to allow the organization to utilize the full amount of the donation in pursuit of its socially redeeming cause.

Conversely, at other times, implementation of the tax laws forces the substance of a transaction to override its form.

> Big Time Bucks Corporation has invested its surplus cash over the years in a portfolio of publicly traded securities. Big Time has had a very profitable year due to the sale of some of the securities in its investment portfolio. Big Time is looking for some year-end tax deductions to shelter some of these profits. In reviewing its portfolio, several securities have lost their value due to a recent overall stock market decline. Big Time thinks these securities will rebound when the market turns around and will eventually appreciate over time. Big Time sells several of these securities at a loss and one week later repurchases the same number of shares of the same companies at approximately the same price at which they were previously sold.

The economic substance of this transaction is that Big Time is in a similar financial position to that which existed prior to its sales at a loss. That is, by buying back the same securities, its portfolio is in the same position financially. The portfolio will perform the same as it would have had the sales not taken place. Because of this, the "wash sales" rules of the Internal Revenue Code (IRC Section 1091) disallow the deduction of the losses against the current year gains. **In this situation, the substance of the transaction overrides the form.**

The preceding examples illustrate two important concepts that the tax researcher should keep in mind when researching the tax consequences of a transaction. First, both fiscal and social policy drive the governing authorities for tax reporting. As such, the required reporting of a transaction for tax purposes may vary from the systematic and rational approach used for financial reporting purposes, often due to fiscal constraints at the time the statutes were enacted. Second, due to the influence of fiscal and social policies, understanding both the form and the substance of any transaction before beginning the research is critical. As one gains experience with the governing tax authorities, familiarity with when and how form or substance controls a situation leads to the ability to provide effective tax planning for a given situation.

In the first two examples we can see that with proper planning, the right structuring of the transaction will maximize the tax deduction and minimize the taxes of Big Time. This is called "tax avoidance" in the terminology of tax planning. Tax avoidance is the legal use of the provisions of the tax law to reduce or minimize tax liability. This concept is different from "tax evasion," which is the illegal reduction of taxes. Some examples of tax evasion include overstating deductions through fictitious or inflated expenses and underreporting or not reporting income.

With respect to tax avoidance, the following quote of Judge Learned Hand is often cited:

> Over and over again courts have said that there is nothing sinister in so arranging
> one's affairs as to keep taxes as low as possible. Everybody does so, rich or poor;
> and all do right, for nobody owes any public duty to pay more than the law
> demands: taxes are enforced extractions, not voluntary contributions. To demand
> more in the name of morals is mere cant.
>
> *Comm. v. Newman*, 47-1 USTC ¶9175, 35 AFTR 857, 159 F.2d
> 848 (CA-2, 1947)

Thus, the objective of good tax planning is to minimize one's taxes while still achieving the desired financial goal of a transaction. This usually requires the careful balancing of these two goals since there are trade-offs between the two. After all, operating a business at a loss will certainly reduce its taxes; but, the business cannot run indefinitely at a loss.

SOURCES OF TAX LAW

In order to find the answer to a tax research problem, one must first know where to look. Over the history of income taxes in the United States, hundreds of thousands of pages of statutes, court cases, administrative pronouncements, and scholarly texts have been compiled on the topic of income taxation. Finding the right source and evaluating it requires a knowledge of the primary and secondary tax sources and their relative weight as authoritative sources.

In this section, the three primary sources of tax information are presented. These three sources correspond with the three branches of our federal government–legislative, administrative, and judicial. In the next section on the citation and location of each of these sources, we discuss both the paper and electronic infobases. Secondary sources are also presented.

Legislative Sources

The House of Representatives and the Senate comprise our legislative branch. Their responsibility is to enact the laws (statutes) that govern our country. Thus, the sources related to the enactment of any tax law, including the statutes themselves, are referred to as *legislative sources*. Laws that encompass federal taxation are contained in the Internal Revenue Code (IRC or often referred to as the Code). Unless the U.S. Supreme Court overturns a specific provision of the Internal Revenue Code as unconstitutional, the provision is the law of the United States. It carries the highest authoritative weight of all tax sources.

Additional legislative sources include the various committee reports that are generated during the legislative process. This process starts with a bill proposed by a member of the House, which is then forwarded for consideration to the House Ways and Means Committee. The Ways and Means Committee reviews the proposed legislation for submission to the full House for debate, modification, and eventual vote.

If approved by the House, the bill is then forwarded to the Senate Finance Committee, which usually modifies the bill to suit the opinions of its members. If the Senate Finance Committee approves the bill, it is then forwarded to the full Senate for additional debate, modification, and vote. After Senate approval, the bill is sent to the Joint Conference Committee on Taxation that is composed of members of both the House and the Senate.

The Joint Conference Committee's duties are to try to reconcile any differences between the bill passed by the House and the one passed by the Senate. This reconciled bill is then sent back to both the House and Senate for a final vote. Assuming both the House and the Senate pass the reconciled bill, it is then sent to the President for his signature. When signed by the President, the bill is called a Revenue Act and is incorporated into the IRC.

Through this process, various reports are prepared that explain the provisions of the legislation, the reasons for their inclusion, as well as the objectives and intent of Congress in enacting the law. For a period of time, these reports are the only explanatory material available to the researcher when dealing with newly enacted provisions. The reports include:

>The House Ways and Means Committee Report,
>House Debate and House Amendments Report,
>The Senate Finance Committee Report,
>Senate Debate and Senate Amendments Report,
>Joint Conference Committee on Taxation Report, and
>Post-Conference Debates Reports.

The Joint Conference Committee on Taxation's report is often referred to as the "Blue Book" since the Government Printing Office traditionally prints the paperback version in a blue cover. It usually contains the original House and Senate committee reports plus the new laws.

The Code is a constantly changing body of law. Obsolete Code sections are repealed and new laws added within the existing structure of the Code. In 1986, the Tax Reform Act was so substantial that the Code was retitled the IRC of 1986 and is the one that is currently updated for each new change in the tax law. The first attempt to organize the existing revenue acts was in 1939. In 1954, a major restructuring of the 1939 IRC occurred, which renumbered the sections. The IRC of 1986 still uses the same numbering system as the IRC of 1954.

The IRC and corresponding committee reports address the U.S. taxation of citizens living in the United States. In addition, Congress passes treaties with other countries regarding the taxation of U.S. citizens working outside the United States and foreign nationals working within the United States. When dealing with such international tax issues, consulting the treaty signed with the related country is necessary.

Although the tax sources addressed in this chapter relate only to U.S. federal taxes, each state has its own set of tax laws that pertain to the income taxation of individuals and businesses located within its boundaries. The research methodology is the same; however, separate reporters and infobases containing the tax laws for each state must be obtained. In addition, state income tax decisions made by the state (as opposed to the federal) system of courts are published in separate volumes.

Legislative Sources

♦   Internal Revenue Code (IRC)
    ♦   Congressional Committee Reports

♦   International Tax Treaties

Administrative Sources

The Treasury Department is the administrative branch of the federal government that is charged with the collection of revenues. The primary source of these revenues is the federal income tax. Within the Treasury Department, the Internal Revenue Service (IRS) is given the task of administering the U.S. federal income tax laws as well as other tax laws such as the federal estate and gift tax.

The IRS must follow the statutes as laid out in the IRC. In carrying out its duties, the IRS issues various types of administrative guidance and procedures for taxpayer use in complying with the law. These pronouncements have varying authoritative weights.

The principal authority issued by the Treasury Department is the regulations. There are various types of regulations with varying authoritative weights. The first type is known as **Statutory Regulations. As the name implies, these regulations carry the same authority as statutes.** Congress specifically authorizes them in the tax law itself. Congress authorizes the Commissioner of the IRS to proscribe regulations for the specific law. Examples of statutory regulations are the regulations governing the filing of consolidated returns.

Consolidated financial statements pose daunting tasks for trained accountants, and Congress did not believe that it was qualified to dictate the detailed law required to accommodate the filing of consolidated tax returns. Thus, the statute merely refers to the requirement that the Commissioner shall proscribe the needed regulations. Such regulations are becoming more commonplace as the tax laws become more complex.

General Regulations are issued to provide additional guidance to taxpayers in interpreting the law. **They represent the IRS's interpretation of specific sections of the law and are just below the Code in authoritative weight.** Although termed permanent, the regulations can be and have been overturned by the courts. Additionally, they may become obsolete due to changes made to the applicable statute. The IRS attempts to remove from the record obsolete regulations by declaring them as such. However, the frequently changing tax laws have made this a formidable task. Therefore, when reading any regulations, it is important to study the applicable IRC sections in effect at the time the regulations were issued in comparison to the current IRC sections. Any changes in the tax law may have significant impact on the validity and interpretation of the regulations.

The next level of regulations is the **Temporary Regulations**. In the normal process of issuing regulations, the IRS drafts proposed regulations, solicits comments, and then reviews them internally with their experts before issuing them. However, sometimes changes in the tax law require immediate issuance of some guidance for taxpayers and the normal review process must be shortened. Such circumstances lead to temporary regulations. **As the name implies, these regulations provide temporary guidance until the IRS has time to finalize the regulations.** By law, temporary regulations expire three years after issuance.

The last type of regulation is the **Proposed Regulations. Proposed regulations carry no authoritative weight since the IRS may revoke them anytime.** As previously mentioned, they are part of the process of creating permanent regulations that are not as time sensitive as to require the issuance of temporary regulations. They are the equivalent of an IRS trial balloon. Often, the IRS will make a request for comments from taxpayers for a certain period following the issuance of proposed regulations. Based on such feedback, the IRS may then rewrite the proposed regulations and issue them as either new proposed or permanent regulations. As a practical matter, even though they have no authoritative weight, taxpayers may find that the proposed regulations are the only guidance available. As such, they provide useful insight into the IRS's position with respect to the tax treatment of a given transaction.

IRS regulations address how a specific section of the IRC is applied. Often, more than one section of the IRC will apply to a given situation. In these cases, the IRS issues **Revenue Rulings. Revenue Rulings show how the IRS applies the law to a given fact pattern**.

Each Revenue Ruling starts with a stipulation of the fact pattern and statement of the applicable sections of the IRC. It then discusses how the law applies and the rationale behind that application. Revenue Rulings are less authoritative than regulations. However, they become more authoritative with the test of time. If a Revenue Ruling has not been challenged or has withstood a judicial challenge of its authority, it gains authoritative weight when compared to a newly issued Revenue Ruling. Also, it is worthwhile to note that IRS personnel are bound to follow Revenue Rulings and do not have the authority to ignore them. Thus, they provide excellent guidance about how the IRS will act if the taxpayer's fact pattern fits the one in a given ruling.

Revenue Procedures are similar to Revenue Rulings with one distinction. **As the name implies, Revenue Procedures deal with administrative procedures with respect to taxpayer rights and duties**. For example, a corporation may wish to change its method of accounting for inventories from FIFO to LIFO. In this situation, the IRS has issued Revenue Procedures that cover the specific steps the taxpayer must follow to get IRS approval to change its accounting method. The Revenue Procedure usually specifies steps, time frames, details of information to be provided, where to file the information, and even specific forms required to be filed.

Finally, various pronouncements carry no authoritative weight but can provide useful insight into the IRS rationale in treating certain situations. These include **Private Letter Rulings (PLR),**

Technical Advice Memoranda (TAM), Actions on Decisions (AOD), and General Counsel Memoranda (GCM).

In a Private Letter Ruling, a taxpayer petitions the IRS to rule on how it would treat a proposed transaction. These are normally done when the area of law is murky and subject to varying interpretations, the dollar amounts are significant to the taxpayer, and the taxpayer desires a specific tax consequence for the transaction to take place. The process for obtaining a PLR is the subject of Revenue Procedures and involves the taxpayer stipulating the facts and the law as he or she interprets it. For a fee, the IRS then provides the taxpayer with a letter indicating how it will treat the transaction based upon the stipulated facts.

The ruling is binding upon the IRS only for the taxpayer who requested it and only for the stipulated fact pattern. The taxpayer does not have to follow through with the transaction if the result is not what is desired. Also, the IRS is not bound to provide the same treatment to subsequent taxpayers even if their facts are identical. For this reason, PLRs do not carry any precedential authority. They provide the IRS's current mode of thought on a particular issue and serve as an insurance policy to taxpayers with significant tax consequences on the line who request the ruling.

Technical Advice Memoranda are similar to PLRs, except in the case of a TAM, it is an employee of the IRS seeking advice for a return currently under audit. The employee requests a ruling from the IRS's legal division on the interpretation of the law with respect to a transaction that has already occurred.

Actions on Decisions are internal IRS memos. They originate from the legal division of the IRS when it has lost in court. **AODs discuss the IRS's position and whether the IRS should appeal its case or walk away.** These memos can be enlightening since the IRS may not appeal a case due to factors other than its interpretation of the law. It may decide that the case was tried in a circuit where it had little support, the dollar value was not significant enough in the given case to appeal, or it may desire a more definitive set of facts if the finding of facts were part of the dispute.

General Counsel Memoranda are issued similar to AODs. **The topics of GCMs consist of the rationale used by the IRS legal division regarding PLRs, TAMs, and Revenue Rulings.** Thus, they have no authoritative weight but do provide valuable insight as to the IRS's current thinking.

Administrative Sources

- ◆ Regulations
  - ◆ Statutory
  - ◆ General
  - ◆ Temporary
  - ◆ Proposed

- ◆ Revenue Rulings

- ◆ Revenue Procedures

- ◆ Pronouncements
  - ◆ Private Letter Rulings
  - ◆ Technical Advice Memorandum
  - ◆ Actions on Decisions
  - ◆ General Counsel Memorandum

Judicial Sources

The U.S. judicial system consists of various court systems across the country. These courts are structured to handle certain types of litigation; therefore, it is necessary to understand the sequence a case takes as it flows through our judicial system.

The courts are categorized as either courts of origin or appellate courts. Courts of origin are the courts where a case is first tried and are also referred to as trial courts. The loser in the court of origin then has the option of appealing the decision to an appellate court. The court to which a case may be appealed depends upon the court in which the case originated. The courts are the final step to be taken if taxpayers and the IRS cannot agree through the normal IRS administrative process.

The U.S. federal court system is divided into numerous districts. Federal District Courts are courts of origin and hear both tax and nontax-related cases. The District Court also is the only court in which a taxpayer can request a trial to be decided by jury. However, juries are limited to questions of fact and cannot decide questions of law. For example, the jury may decide whether a person did or did not use corporate property for personal use–a question of fact. The jury cannot decide whether the personal use of corporate property results in taxable income since that is a question of law.

A District Court decision is binding only within the district it is decided. It is possible for the same facts to be tried in different districts and have different decisions rendered. Thus, any time a District Court decision is used in tax research, the researcher must be careful to note in which district it was decided. Preferably, one would want a District Court decision in the same jurisdiction as that of the taxpayer. Before litigating in the District Court, the taxpayer must first pay the tax and then sue for a refund. The loser in a District Court case may appeal his or her case to the U.S. Circuit Court of Appeals in which the District Court resides.

The U.S. Tax Court is another court of origin. Unlike other federal courts, the Tax Court hears only tax related cases. The court consists of judges who travel the country to hear tax disputes at predetermined times and locations. The Tax Court judges are usually more knowledgeable in matters of tax than other court judges due to the Tax Court's specialization in tax cases. This expertise is significant when the issue involved is one of technical interpretation as opposed to a question of fact. It is the only court in which the taxpayer may litigate without first paying the tax and then suing for a refund.

Since the U.S. Tax Court hears many cases across the country, it issues two types of decisions. These are "regular" decisions and "memorandum" decisions. Regular decisions are issued when the Tax Court hears a case in which the facts or issues are new and distinguishable from other cases it has previously heard. Memorandum decisions are issued when the Tax Court hears a case in which the facts and issues are repetitive and indistinguishable from a case it has previously decided. In the memorandum decision, the Tax Court notes that the facts and issues are similar to the prior cases and that nothing new has arisen in the interim to change its decision or the application of the relevant law. Thus, regular decisions and memorandum decisions have the same authoritative weight for all practical purposes. The difference is merely in the way they are labeled.

Before 1943, the U.S. Tax Court was known as the Board of Tax Appeals. It was an administrative board of the Treasury Department rather than a true judicial court. Today, Tax Court cases may be appealed to the Circuit Court of Appeals in which the Tax Court decision was made. For this reason, the U.S. Tax Court must follow the decisions of the Circuit Court of Appeals in which it is hearing cases.

The U.S. Claims Court is another court of origin. It is responsible for hearing cases involving any monetary claims against the United States government. Before October 1, 1982, this court was known as the U.S. Court of Claims. Just like the District Court, the Claims Court hears both tax and nontax claims and the taxpayer must first pay the tax and sue for a refund. Similar to the U.S. Tax Court, the Claims Court is based in Washington, D.C., but judges travel the circuits to hear cases throughout the country. However, since Claims Court decisions are appealed to the U.S. Court of Appeals for the Federal Circuit, the Claims Court is not bound by the geographical Court of Appeals in which it is hearing the case. Cases prior to October 1982 that were tried in the predecessor U.S. Court of Claims were appealed to the U.S. Supreme Court.

There are thirteen Circuit Courts of Appeal. Eleven cover the fifty states, one covers Washington, D.C. and the other was created in October 1982 to hear appeals from the U.S. Claims Court. Each geographical circuit is referred to by its number (e.g., the Seventh Circuit Court, CA-7) and contains various District Courts within its geographic boundaries. The Circuit Courts hear only cases on appeal from their respective District Courts and U.S. Tax Court cases that were tried within their boundaries. Circuit Courts hear both tax and nontax cases. The decisions of Circuit Courts are binding on the circuit in which they were decided. The decisions of the Circuit Courts may be appealed only to the U.S. Supreme Court.

The U.S. Supreme Court has the duty of upholding the Constitution of the United States. Although cases can be appealed to the Supreme Court, the court selects only a few tax cases to hear. The Supreme Court focuses its work on cases involving whether a law or its application is within the spirit of the Constitution. As such, the Supreme Court rarely hears tax cases unless they involve issues about the constitutionality of a particular statute or administrative pronouncement (Regulations, etc.). Since the Supreme Court can declare a law unconstitutional, and thereby unenforceable, it can overrule the IRC. It is the final interpretation of the law. U.S. Supreme Court decisions are binding on all taxpayers and the IRS despite the geographical location of the origin of the case.

Judicial Sources

♦   U.S. Supreme Court

    ♦   Circuit Court of Appeals
        ♦   U.S. Tax Court
        ♦   Federal District Courts

    ♦   U.S. Court of Appeals for the Federal Circuit
        ♦   U.S. Claims Court

CITATION AND LOCATION OF TAX SOURCES

All three types of primary sources can be found on an electronic infobase such as *CCH Access* or *RIA OnPoint System*. These two infobases are reproductions of CCH's tax service entitled the *Standard Federal Tax Reports* and RIA's tax service entitled the *U.S. Federal Tax Reporter*. They may be purchased as a series of monthly CD-ROMs or online. The online service is more expensive because it is updated daily. These services are not currently available on the Internet. As an example, we reproduce the main menu of the *RIA OnPoint System* in Exhibit 7-1.

Similar to FARS, it uses Folio Bound VIEWS as its search and retrieval software. By double-clicking on the "Code, Regs, Com Rpts, Legislation" icon, we can see its table of contents. The legislative sources may be found here along with the Treasury Regulations. Note that icons for the IRC and Regulations are also located at the bottom of the screen.

The other administrative sources previously discussed can be found under "IRS Pubs, Rulings, Releases, Tables." The "Federal Court Decisions and Citator" file contains the judicial sources. Additional sources that are available on the system are subsequently discussed under the section entitled "Tax Research Methodology."

Relevant sources may be accessed by searching the files using keywords or by retrieving a specific document directly using the search submenu. To use these infobases effectively, the researcher needs to know how to construct and interpret references for the various tax sources. These references are known as citations and follow specific formats. Understanding these formats allows the researcher to find the authority to read and evaluate firsthand.

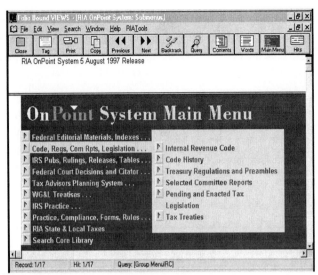

EXHIBIT 7-1

In the following sections, we discuss citations for the legislative, administrative, and judicial sources. We then provide instructions for finding the cited sources in both the paper and electronic services.

Legislative Sources

The statutory source for tax law is the Internal Revenue Code. The IRC is organized into the following divisions (greatest to least):

> Subtitles
> Chapters
> Subchapters
> Parts
> Subparts
> Sections
> Subsections
> Paragraphs
> Subparagraphs
> Clauses

The above structure must be kept in mind when reading the IRC. Some provisions state that a particular law applies only "for the purposes of this subtitle" or some other division. Thus, it is necessary to know how the IRC is structured in order to understand how broad or narrow a provision or definition may be applied.

While the IRC contains numerous levels, the normal citation for a given provision usually starts at the section level. Each section number is unique and displayed in numerical order. Different transactions are often referred to by the applicable Code section. Cites for the IRC follow this format:

> IRC 381(c)(1)(C)(iv)

This would read:

> Section 381, Subsection c, Paragraph 1, Subparagraph C, Clause iv.

Publishing companies such as Commerce Clearing House (CCH) and the Research Institute of America (RIA) reproduce the IRC in either one- or two-volume paperback editions. A topical index is also included to help the researcher pinpoint the applicable section number in the IRC.

As previously discussed, the IRC can also be easily accessed on the computer. By going to the main menu of either *CCH Access* or *RIA OnPoint System*, the IRC file can be retrieved. This infobase can then be researched by specifying keywords or, if known, the section number citation. A separate tax service containing all of the tax treaties not only is available in the traditional paper tax treaty services but also is reproduced as a separate file on the electronic infobase.

Administrative Sources

Citations for Regulations follow a format similar to the citation for the IRC. For example:

> Reg. Sec. 1.46-1(a)

When reading the citation for a regulation, noticing several things is important. The first part of the description, **Reg.**, indicates that this is a permanent regulation. **Temp. Reg.** indicates a temporary regulation and a capital **T** appears in the citation. A proposed regulation is designated by **Prop. Reg.**

The second portion of the citation (1.46) indicates two things. The **1.** designates that this is an **income** tax regulation. Other commonly seen numbers include:

20–Estate taxes
25–Gift taxes
31–Employment taxes
301–Procedural matters

The number following this designation indicates that the regulation relates to IRC Section 46. This number will always correspond to the related IRC section. However, subsequent divisions following the section number do not correspond directly to the related subsection, paragraph, subparagraph, and clause numbers in the IRC.

CCH and RIA each reproduce the Treasury Regulations in a multivolume paperback set. A keyword topical index is also included. The permanent and temporary regulations are merged together in numerical sequence throughout the volumes. The proposed regulations are set aside in a separate section located at the end.

In the same manner as the IRC, the regulations may be accessed on the computer by retrieving the file containing the regulations from the main menu of the electronic database (e.g., *CCH Access* or *RIA OnPoint System*). A search of the regulations may be made by specifying applicable keywords or the regulation citation.

Revenue Rulings (Rev. Rul.) and Revenue Procedures (Rev. Proc.) follow a similar citation format. Since they are both published twice a year, once in the weekly *Internal Revenue Bulletin* (IRB) and then subsequently in the *Cumulative Bulletin* (CB), they will have two different citations. The first is called a temporary citation and is used until the related CB is released. Once the CB is released, the permanent citation is used.

The following is an example of a temporary citation:

> Rev. Rul. 85-3, 1985-2 IRB 4

This citation shows that the Revenue Ruling was the third Revenue Ruling issued in 1985 **(Rev. Rul. 85-3)**. It can be found in the second weekly *Internal Revenue Bulletin* issued in 1985 beginning on page 4 **(1985-2 IRB 4)**. Permanent citations are used once the CB is published and follow the same format:

> Rev. Proc. 84-85, 1984-2 CB 118

This is the permanent citation for the eighty-fifth Revenue Procedure issued in 1984 **(Rev. Proc. 84-85)**. It can be found in the second volume of the 1984 CB beginning on page 118 **(1984-2 CB 118)**.

The IRB is the official voice of the IRS. Twice a year, the IRBs are organized according to Code section and published as a CB (so named since the CBs are an accumulation of the previous weekly bulletins). In addition to the Revenue Rulings and Procedures, the IRBs (CBs) contain new regulations (called Treasury Decisions), revenue acts and corresponding congressional committee reports, and tax treaties. The CBs are published by the Printing Office and are reproduced in the electronic tax infobases. Once again, if the researcher knows the citation, he or she may immediately retrieve the referenced document. If not, a keyword search can always be used.

Private Letter Rulings (PLR) and Technical Advice Memoranda (TAM) use a similar citation format. The first two numbers indicate the year the item was issued, the next two numbers show the week it was issued, and the final three numbers tell which number it was during the week of issue. An example of each pronouncement and its interpretation follows:

PLR 8242001–first PLR issued during the forty-second week of 1982.

TAM 8426014–fourteenth TAM issued during the twenty-sixth week of 1984.

PLRs and TAMs are merged in numerical order and contained in a separate file on each of the electronic infobases. They may be accessed through a keyword search or by designation of the proper citation.

Judicial Sources

Judicial citations follow a general pattern:

> *Name of case*, Volume number REPORTER page or paragraph number (court, year of decision)

The REPORTER is the name of the court case reporting service being used. The primary reporters for all federal tax cases except those decided in the U.S. Tax Court are CCH's *United States Tax Cases* (USTC) and RIA's *American Federal Tax Reports* (AFTR or AFTR2d). Regular U.S. Tax Court decisions are published in the *Tax Court of the United States Reports* (TC) and memorandum decisions are reproduced in a separate series such as CCH's *U.S. Tax Court Memorandums* (TCM).

Depending on the reporter, the citation may refer to either the page number (AFTR, AFTR2d, TC, TCM) while others may use the paragraph number (USTC). The court abbreviations are District Courts (D. Ct. IL), Claims Court (Cls. Ct. since 1982, Ct. Cls. for earlier decisions), Fifth Circuit Court of Appeals (CA-5), or Supreme Court (USSC or Sup. Ct.) The following examples of different court citations by different reporters show the varying formats.

U.S. Supreme Court

Helvering v. Horst, 24 AFTR 1058 (Sup. Ct., 1940)
Helvering v. Horst, 40-1 USTC ¶9787 (Sup. Ct., 1940)

Circuit Court of Appeals

Stanford v. Commissioner, 8 AFTR2d 5763 (CA-9 1961)
Stanford v. Commissioner, 61-2 USTC ¶9724 (CA-9 1961)

U.S. Claims Court

Glover Packing Co. of Texas v. U.S., 13 AFTR2d 632 (Ct. Cls. 1964)
Glover Packing Co. of Texas v. U.S., 64-1 USTC ¶9249 (Ct. Cls. 1964)

Federal District Courts

Louisville Trust Co., Executor v. Glenn, 25 AFTR 464 (W.D. Ky. 1940)
Louisville Trust Co., Executor v. Glenn, 42 USTC ¶9514 (W.D. Ky. 1940)

U.S. Tax Court

W.C. Grammam, 46 TC 1 (1966)   Regular decision
Landpheir, James, TC Memo 1981-145   Memorandum decision

A large tax library will contain these tax reporters in hardbound volumes. However, due to space constraints, the tax practitioner may have these cases at his or her fingertips via the computer. Each of the electronic infobases contains all of the court cases and stores them for use in separate files. If we know the proper citation, we can immediately retrieve a case. If not, a keyword search is an alternative.

Exercise 7-1   Name: _____

Locating Legislative Sources   Section: _____

Instructions: Locate each of the following legislative sources using an electronic tax infobase.
Briefly answer the corresponding questions.

1. IRC 11   If a corporation's taxable income is $80,000 for the current year, what is its tax
              liability?

_____

2. IRC 162(a) Which two criteria must be met for expenses to be deductible in a trade or
               business?

_____

_____

3. IRC 195   What is a "start-up expenditure?"

_____

_____

              How can it be deducted?

_____

_____

4. IRC 197   If a corporation purchases a business and pays for goodwill, can the corporation
              deduct the cost of goodwill?

_____

_____

              If so, specify the time period over which the cost may be deducted.

_____

_____

5. IRC 248   What is a corporate organizational expenditure?

_____

_____

6. IRC 448   Under what conditions can a corporation use the cash-basis method of accounting?

_____

_____

7. Mexico Income Tax Treaty   When was the treaty signed?

_____

8. Joint Conference Committee   What is the name of the Revenue Act which added this
   Report on IRC 197   section?
   (as first enacted)

_____

What is the Public Law (PL) number assigned to this Act?

_____

When was the Act signed into law?

_____

Exercise 7-2   Name: _____
Locating Administrative Sources   Section: _____

Instructions: Locate each of the following administrative sources using an electronic tax infobase. Briefly answer the corresponding questions.

1. Reg. 1.197-1T

IRC 197 was enacted on August 10, 1993. This temporary regulation allows an election to be made for treating property acquired before this date according to new law requirements. With respect to what date can this election be retroactively applied?

_____

_____

2. Reg. 1.248-1

When does a corporation begin business for the purpose of amortizing organizational expenses?

_____

_____

3. Rev. Rul. 87-41, 1987-1 CB 296

What is the overriding criterion for determining whether a worker is an employee or a self-employed individual?

_____

_____

4. Rev. Proc. 95-10, 1995-1 CB 501

What is the purpose of this Revenue Procedure?

_____

_____

_____

5. PLR 9401014

In this Private Letter Ruling, the IRS addresses the tax treatment of a corporation that converts to a general partnership. What are the last two sentences in this ruling (before "Sincerely yours")?

_____

_____

Exercise 7-3   **Name:** _____
Locating Judicial Sources   **Section:** _____

***Instructions: Locate each of the following court cases using an electronic tax infobase.
Briefly answer the corresponding questions.***

1. *Welch*, 12 AFTR 1456, 3 USTC ¶1164 (USSC, 1933)

    Which court heard this case?

    _____

    In which court did this case originate?

    _____

    To which Circuit Court was this case appealed?

    _____

    Briefly summarize the facts, issues, and decision. (Note that Welch was heard before the
    codification of all Revenue Acts in 1939.)

    _____

    _____

    _____

    _____

2. *H.L. Jenkins*, TC Memo 1983-667, 47 CCH TCM 238

    Which court heard this case?

    _____

    Where did the taxpayer live?

    _____

    Why did the Court allow Jenkins (Conway Twitty) to deduct his payments to investors as
    ordinary and necessary business expenses in light of the decision in *Welch*?

    _____

    _____

    _____

    _____

INTERNET SERVICES

With the rapid growth of both users and available information on the Internet, researchers should not overlook the opportunity to locate useful information on the Internet. Due to its constantly changing nature, listing all the available sources of tax information currently available on the Internet would be impossible. Some sites come and go or move to different servers. However, most Web browsers utilize search engines that use Boolean logic. Thus, finding potential Web sites can be done using these search engines and a well-constructed Boolean search. For the reader's reference, the following two sites are well established and not as likely to change. Both sites contain a wealth of information and links to many other tax-related sites on the Internet.

http://law.house.gov/109.htm

This site is the United States House of Representatives' Web page that contains information regarding the tax laws of all the states as well as federal taxation. It has links to state statutes, regulations, tax forms, cases, and other state tax-related information. Additionally, it has links to the IRS home page and the IRC, Regulations, forms, publications, and other administrative sources. The IRS site has a keyword search engine to help in finding information.

http://www.yahoo.com/Government/Taxes/

Yahoo.com is a commercial Web site that provides links to various Web sites. It is structured by various categories and the above link takes you to its page that has links to various tax-related Web sites. These include federal, state, and even some foreign tax sources. This page also does not limit itself to income taxes; estate and gift taxes, sales taxes, and tax planning sites are also available. In addition, many accounting firms now have Web sites and links to some of them can also be found here.

TAX RESEARCH METHODOLOGY

With a basic understanding of the three sources of tax law, we can now perform tax research. Authoritative sources can be classified into two categories: primary and secondary. Primary authorities are the items previously discussed under the headings of legislative, administrative, and judicial sources. If the researcher knows the citation for a particular document, he or she can retrieve it directly from the tax service infobase. However, this is generally not the case and the researcher usually begins the research process with secondary sources.

Secondary sources consist of narratives that discuss the statutes, administrative pronouncements, and court cases. Examples include textbooks, journals, magazines, newsletters, and editorial commentaries and explanations. Most practitioners consider the tax services to be the most useful secondary source for doing research. We discuss use of the tax services in the following sections.

Secondary sources merely present the authors' interpretation of the relevant primary authorities. As such, they are not authoritative from the standpoint of being used as legal precedent for taking a position with regard to the proper tax treatment of a transaction. However, they are a very good source for obtaining background knowledge and generating keywords regarding areas in which the researcher is unfamiliar.

Tax Research Steps

Organization is the key to doing productive and efficient tax research. With the myriad of sources available, it is possible to lose focus on your search and wander aimlessly through countless pages of information. The researcher needs to focus on the problem at hand by using an effective methodology. The tax research methodology can be broken down into the following six steps:

1. Understand the problem.
2. Formulate a research strategy.
3. Search the applicable sources.
4. Evaluate the authorities.
5. Document the research.
6. Update the research.

Understand the Problem. While this may seem to be a simplistic statement, it is not so when the examples illustrating charitable contributions at the beginning of this chapter are reviewed. The tax researcher must always keep in mind that tax laws vary with respect to the effect of relevance of form versus substance on the outcome of a given transaction. Understanding the problem means understanding both the form and the substance of a given transaction.

The starting point is getting the facts. This task is much like detective work in that some facts may later be deemed irrelevant while other information may need to be obtained as the researcher explores the tax laws. Before beginning any research problem, list as many facts as possible. Some things to keep in mind are:

The parties involved and their relationships to each other;

The sequence of events that form the underlying transaction;

What is being transferred (services, inventory, etc.); and

Any obligations of the parties (either prior to the transaction or subsequent to the transaction such as options to buy, requirements to sell, minimum payments, etc.).

As a researcher becomes more knowledgeable about the law, this part becomes easier. For instance, stock ownership percentages of shareholders are important factors in most transactions involving a shareholder and the corporation or other shareholders. At what level of ownership stock percentage becomes significant varies depending on the IRC section involved. For some laws stock ownership can affect the tax outcome at levels as low as five percent while others may require fifty percent or greater. Also, ownership is defined for some provisions as direct ownership while other provisions include the stock of certain relatives or other business entities in which the shareholder may have an ownership interest. This can seem overwhelming to the novice, but with experience it becomes easier.

A helpful tool for understanding the transaction is to diagram the transaction. It is often said "a picture is worth a thousand words," and in tax research a picture can save many hours that might otherwise be spent on researching the wrong issue. The diagram can be done with flowcharts or sketched using stick figures with boxes and circles to represent the parties, and numbered lines with arrows showing the flow of items and the sequence of events. If a researcher cannot easily diagram a transaction (consideration of artistic talent aside), then he or she probably does not have a solid grasp of the facts of the situation. Until a diagram can be done, the researcher should not continue. If the facts are not right, one cannot hope to achieve a proper result. By restructuring the parties or sequence of events, often a desirable result can be achieved or an undesirable result avoided.

Formulate a Research Strategy. Once we have gathered the facts and defined the issues, a keyword list should be developed. It should contain key terms, or identified issues, and known IRC sections, regulations, or related materials. It is prepared from the list of facts and a review of the diagram. As previously mentioned, there are various tax services that a researcher can use when looking for a solution and all have one thing in common. They all provide entry to the services' thousands of pages via use of keywords, IRC sections, regulations, rulings, and cases, or some combination of these.

A keyword list helps to insure that one starts at the correct point and that the researcher does not forget to review a given point. Points on the list can be checked off as they are researched. Also, we can expand the list as new keywords are discovered during the research process.

Search the Applicable Sources. With a keyword list in hand, the researcher can then begin a review of the authoritative sources. If the researcher is familiar with the topics to be researched, then the starting point will be the primary sources such as the IRC, regulations, court cases, and so on. As previously discussed, if the researcher knows the applicable citations, the documents can easily be retrieved from the stacks or on the computer.

Often, the researcher does not know what the relevant tax sources are. In these cases, he or she may use keywords to search through each file on the computer or use topical indices to search the hardbound volumes of the Code, regulations, CBs, and the like. This route generally is inefficient and tedious. Fortunately, the large tax services such as CCH's *Standard Federal Tax Reports* and RIA's *U.S. Federal Tax Reporter* have already organized the tax sources according to IRC section. **With respect to each section in the IRC, the editors of the tax services reproduce the law and provide commentaries and brief summaries of relevant tax sources. The summaries are called annotations and the formal citation for each primary tax source is also provided.**

The electronic reproductions of these tax services, *CCH Access* and *RIA OnPoint System*, contain these explanations and annotations as well. The contents for the icon "Federal Editorial Materials, Indexes" for *RIA OnPoint System* is shown in Exhibit 7-2.

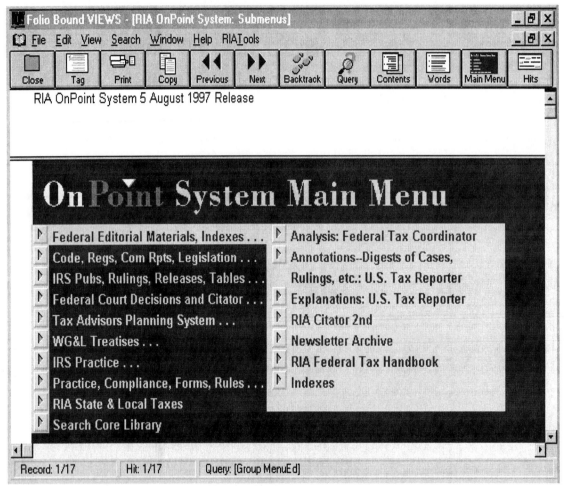

EXHIBIT 7-2

Note that there is a separate file for Annotations and for Explanations contained in the *U.S. Tax Reporter*. Both files are organized according to IRC section and may be searched using keywords or specific citations for the primary tax sources. The annotations briefly summarize individual court cases, IRS rulings, and other documents that pertain to a specific IRC section. The explanations are the editors' commentaries with respect to a particular law. In addition, *RIA OnPoint System* has a second tax service entitled the *Federal Tax Coordinator* (*FTC*), which is organized according to subject matter. It also contains editorial explanations and citations to primary sources relating to a particular topic.

Often, a researcher begins with one of these three files when he or she is unfamiliar with the tax law and does not know the citation of a primary source concerning the issue. Note that the icons for each of these three files are reproduced at the bottom of the screen that emphasizes their utility.

When using any service, it is necessary to distinguish between the primary authorities and the commentary of the service's publisher, which is a secondary authority. The commentary is the opinion of the publisher's editorial board and should never be cited. **A researcher cannot substitute a publisher's opinion for the researcher's own professional judgment.** As a researcher, one must form his or her own opinion based on his or her reading of the primary authorities. This does not mean to imply that publishers are wrong or incompetent. After all, the service has probably been around for many years and the publishers are experts in their fields. If the researcher disagrees with the opinion of the publisher, he or she should be able to show what primary authority supports his or her position.

In summary, with respect to studying the applicable tax sources, the researcher's familiarity with the topic determines the starting point of research. When the researcher has a good comfort level with the topic, the starting point is the primary sources. If the researcher is unfamiliar or does not have sufficient experience in the area, the starting point is the secondary sources. After gathering sufficient background information from the secondary sources, the researcher should then update the facts list, transaction diagram, and keyword list. With these updated items, the researcher can then proceed to use the tax services to locate the relevant primary sources.

Evaluate the Authorities. In the earlier part of this chapter, we discussed the various primary sources of the tax law and their relative authoritative weights. When researching tax issues, the researcher must keep in mind that all three sources may not exist for a given item. There may be no regulations or court case for a specific transaction. Thus, the researcher looks at the sources that can be found and weighs each based upon its relative authoritative weight.

Sometimes conflicting court decisions may appear and the researcher is forced to analyze which one he or she thinks is more substantial. Some factors to consider when evaluating court cases are the following:

> 1. *Similarity of facts.* Oftentimes, the sources may not be identical ("on point" in the tax research vernacular) but may require some analogy to be drawn between the given facts and the available authorities. The researcher must use his or her professional judgment to evaluate the relative importance of the facts that agree versus those that do not.

> 2. *Level and jurisdiction of the court.* A U.S. Supreme Court decision overrides all other decisions. If two Circuit Courts disagree, then each court's decision is controlling in its circuit. If a client is in neither jurisdiction, then the tax researcher must consider decisions of the U.S. Tax Court, Court of Claims, and District Court rendered to other taxpayers in the client's jurisdiction. If two district courts of the same circuit disagree, the matter will usually be appealed to the Circuit Court. The U.S. Tax Court is bound by law to follow any decisions of the Circuit Court in which the client resides.

> 3. *Recency of the court case.* In general, all things considered, the more recent the court case, the more likely the decision will be followed in a subsequent case.

Document the Research. Once the authorities have been evaluated and the conclusions reached, the researcher should then document the work before communicating it to the user. This should be done in the form of a written memorandum. The suggested format of such memorandum should take its form and flow from the research process.

A well-written memorandum begins with a heading that consists of four entries: (1) the name of the person to whom the memo is addressed, (2) the name of the person who wrote the memo, (3) the date, and (4) an entry identifying the client and the issue or issues discussed in the memorandum.

In the second section, the relevant facts should be stated. All significant facts should be included and organized chronologically or topically. Present the facts accurately and objectively. After all, if these are not correct up front, the rest of the memorandum is irrelevant since it will not address the user's concerns or problems.

In the third section, the tax issues should be specified in a concise manner. When possible, applicable IRC sections should be included.

In the fourth section, the relevant primary authorities on which we base the conclusions should be cited and discussed, beginning with the applicable law and regulations. If the statute is long and complicated, quote the relevant sections and then paraphrase. Relevant cases and rulings should be cited and discussed with respect to how the law has been interpreted and applied. Significant differences between the fact patterns found in court cases, Revenue Rulings, and so forth, and the client's situation should be noted. In addition, the researcher should discuss how conflicting authorities are resolved. This is the longest section because it contains all the primary authorities that support the conclusions and a discussion of their relative strengths and weaknesses. We should never cite secondary authorities.

The last part of the memorandum contains the conclusions and any recommendations. These should logically flow from the discussions in the prior two parts. This section should also include an emphasis on any time-sensitive or special actions that may be required to achieve the desired results such as required deadlines, forms or information to be filed, specific steps to be taken, and the consequences of failing to meet such requirements.

These items are necessary to communicate effectively to the user what has to be done. The number one cause for professional liability litigation is a failure to communicate between the parties. This failure leads to inappropriate actions by one party (usually the user of the information), who typically bases his or her suit on the "you didn't tell me" premise. By proper documentation in the written memorandum format, there is no question as to what was told. It is the researcher's professional obligation to be sure that all relevant information is contained in the memorandum and to follow up to be sure that it is properly understood.

Update the Research. The last step before sending the written memorandum to the client should be a final update of all information contained in the facts and authorities used. This is paramount since the tax law is changing daily with new laws, regulations and rulings, and cases. Different paper tax services are updated daily, weekly, monthly, or some other period. They all have different ways in which they are updated, varying from separate pages referencing the changed pages to the replacement of the pages.

With respect to electronic services, the update is usually in the form of a new CD or diskette that usually comes out monthly. If the tax service is online, it is updated daily. Whichever form it takes, the service will have instructions on how to be sure you are using the most up-to-date information available. Use of information more than a week old can be dangerous in the quickly changing tax environment.

Court cases should be updated using a special tax service known as a citator. The citator is available in hardbound paper volumes and is also maintained in a separate file in the electronic tax service infobases. In the citator, the history of each case is presented along with a list of subsequent cases that have cited it. A good citator allows the researcher to see whether subsequent cases have confirmed, differentiated, or overturned the cited case. Also, cases may involve more than one issue. The researcher must review the cases to decide if the reason for the citation was the issue he or she is addressing or some other issue. In addition, the citator is useful for determining whether Revenue Rulings and Revenue Procedures are still valid.

Tax Research Methodology

- **Understand the Problem**
  - List the known facts
  - Diagram the transaction for form and substance

- **Formulate a Research Strategy**

- **Search the Applicable Sources**
  - Primary sources–start here if familiar with subject
  - Secondary sources–start here if unfamiliar with subject

- **Evaluate the Authorities**
  - Relative weights of primary authorities
  - Similarity of facts to your case
  - Level and jurisdiction of court cases
  - Recency of the primary authorities

- **Document the Research**
  - Heading
  - Statement of relevant facts
  - Issues identified
  - Relevant primary authorities discussed/explained
  - Conclusions and recommendations including action steps to be taken

- **Update the Research**
  - Use most recent information available
  - Citator
    - Court Cases
    - Revenue Rulings and Revenue Procedures
  - Cross-reference tables for other primary authorities

Exercise 7-4   Name: _____
Locating Tax Sources Using Keywords   Section: _____

Instructions: Using the following case information, complete the worksheet questions below.

Target Inc., a large manufacturing corporation, was publicly held and traded on the New York Stock Exchange. During the year, it was acquired by another corporation in a friendly takeover. The merger was structured as a tax-free transaction.

Target Inc. incurred both legal and investment banking fees. The investment banking firm was paid to value the stock, render a fairness opinion, and be ready to assist if there was a hostile takeover attempt.

The issue is whether the takeover expenses are deductible as ordinary and necessary business expenses under Section 162 or capital expenditures under Section 263.

Part 1. Generate a list of keywords to research this issue.

_____   _____

_____   _____

_____   _____

Part 2. Go to the electronic tax infobases and perform a keyword search on the tax service's explanations and annotations (e.g., RIA USTR explanations, RIA USTR Annotations, *RIA Federal Tax Coordinator, CCH Federal Income Tax Reporter*). List the paragraph numbers of the tax services that appear applicable. (Remember, these paragraph numbers are not authoritative cites and should not be used in your memorandum.)

_____   _____

_____   _____

_____   _____

_____   _____

Part 3.   List the primary tax sources that are cited in the above paragraphs.

_____   _____

_____   _____

_____   _____

Part 4. One case that you might have cited in Part 3 is *A.E. Staley Manufacturing Co., et. al.,* 105 TC 166 (1995). Read this case and locate it in the citator.

        (a)   Which court heard this case?

                      _____

        (b)   In which jurisdiction (state) is Staley located?

                      _____

        (c)   Has this case been appealed?

                      _____

        (d)   Have any subsequent cases cited *Staley* favorably?

                      _____

        (e)   Briefly summarize the court's findings in *Staley*.

_____

_____

_____

_____

Part 5. Write a brief recommendation advising Target Inc. how its expenses should be treated.

_____

_____

_____

_____

_____

_____

_____

_____

_____

COMPARISON OF PAPER AND ELECTRONIC TAX SERVICES

It must be emphasized at this point that the research process is the same regardless of whether the paper or the electronic tax service is used. If the researcher knows the citations for the documents he or she needs, it is merely a question as to whether the researcher prefers to locate the hardbound volume in the library or find the file containing that document on the computer. One comparative advantage of using the computer is that when a document refers to another tax source, the researcher can merely click on the cite and immediately link to the cited case, Revenue Ruling, or other associated source. The ability to retrieve documents quickly saves time.

If the researcher does not know which documents are applicable to his or her situation, he or she must begin with a keyword search. This search may be performed by using the topical word index available in the paper tax services such as CCH's *Standard Federal Tax Reports* or RIA's *U.S. Federal Tax Reporter* and RIA's *Tax Coordinator.* Once the topic has been found in the service, primary sources are cited that the researcher can locate.

Alternatively, each of these tax services is reproduced electronically by CCH and RIA and is available in a separate file contained in *CCH's Access* and *RIA's OnPoint System* infobases. Using a keyword search, the researcher should arrive at the same point, finding the same references and citations as in the paper tax services. He or she then merely links to the documents that are applicable.

Clearly, use of the electronic infobases by a tax practitioner who is knowledgeable and experienced in a given area can save time. The updating process and use of the citator may require checking multiple cross-referencing tables and volumes in the paper tax service; whereas, if the tax researcher has access to an online electronic tax service, tax sources and the citator are immediately updated on a daily basis. This benefit is of tremendous value to the tax researcher.

Many tax practitioners and students use both the paper and electronic tax services. Oftentimes, they initially start with the paper product to hone in on keywords and the magnitude of the tax sources involved in researching a particular issue. Then they go to the computer and use the keywords to retrieve the editorial material, link quickly to the cited primary authorities and scan for relevancy, print instead of photocopy relevant documents, and receive automatically updated sources. Use of both the paper and electronic tax services provides a check on the comprehensiveness, accuracy, and currency of the research.

THE CORPORATE INCOME TAX–A FRAMEWORK

In order to do tax research, one needs to have a background for understanding the issue. An individual cannot research in a vacuum. The research cases developed for this chapter address corporate tax issues. It is highly recommended that students read a chapter in a textbook (a secondary tax source) concerning the fundamentals of corporate taxation. The following guidelines may help with the research cases at the end of the chapter.

The U.S. federal government levies a tax on the *income* of corporations. The basic formula for computing taxable corporate income is gross income minus deductions. If a corporation has gross receipts that exceed, on average, $5,000,000 during the prior three years, it must use the accrual method of accounting for reporting income for tax purposes. (Otherwise, the corporation may elect a cash-basis method of reporting.) Thus, many items reported for tax purposes follow GAAP; however, there are a number of differences.

For financial purposes, the full amount of the expense is generally subtracted from income. However, an issue that continuously arises in tax audits and the courts is whether an expense is reasonable, ordinary, and necessary for conducting business and should be allowed as a deduction for tax purposes under Section 162.

In addition, the tax law limits the amount of certain expenses that may be deducted. For example, only fifty percent of the meals and entertainment expense incurred by a corporation is deductible for tax purposes. Other tax limitations apply to such items as deductions for charitable contributions, pension contributions, and losses on the sale of investments (capital assets).

Different rules apply for financial and tax purposes regarding which costs must be capitalized and which costs may be currently expensed or deducted. If capitalization is required under the tax rules, rigid laws dictate the time period over which the asset may be depreciated or amortized. Timing differences between financial and tax reporting are created.

In addition, permanent differences also arise. For example, the tax law allows a deduction for dividends received by a corporation on its investments. Also, interest received by a corporation on its investment in state and local bonds is not taxable.

A knowledge of GAAP is helpful with respect to understanding the substance of the transaction but cannot be relied upon to dictate its tax treatment. A knowledge of both the financial and tax reporting requirements is necessary for the financial accountant who must audit the deferred tax account on the balance sheet as well as the tax practitioner who must reconcile financial and taxable income on the corporate tax return (Form 1120, Schedule M-1).

The tax accountant must research each transaction with respect not only to the amount of the income that must be included and the amount of the expense that may be deducted, but also he or she must determine in what year each item should be reported on the tax return. In practice, the tax accountant will usually work with the financial trial balances of the corporation and make adjustments to arrive at the corporate taxable net income amount.

The corporate tax rate structure is progressive with the highest marginal tax rate set at thirty five percent. This means that approximately one third of a multimillion dollar corporation's net income may be paid out in corporate taxes. Tax is a large corporate cost. No wonder good tax researchers who can find ways to minimize a corporation's taxes are in great demand!

Sample Research Case

The following paragraphs contain an illustration of the research process as it relates to a given set of facts. The next section presents an illustration of the corresponding research memorandum.

Dirtdigger, Inc. is engaged in the business of waste collection and disposal. It began business in 1980 with two garbage trucks. Today, this business is incorporated with an annual revenue of about $10,000,000.

Dirtdigger is considering expanding and plans to pay $3,000,000 for landfills located fairly close to Chicago. It estimates that the salvage value of these acres upon termination of use as a landfill is about $500,000. Dirtdigger would like to know how this expenditure should be treated for tax purposes.

In this case, a substantial amount of money is at stake. Anna, the tax practitioner, knows that land is not depreciable under the tax laws. However, she tells the client that she will research the issue and see if there is any way the $3,000,000 may be capitalized and written off over time.

Anna knows that she is dealing with an issue in a specific industry and believes there must be a number of tax sources that address this situation. She begins her research with the keywords *landfill*, *garbage*, *depreciation*, and *depletion*. Anna then selects a tax service from a file on the electronic infobase and types in the keywords. In this case, the keyword *landfill* has proven to be most productive.

The editorial comments in the tax service explain that several court cases have held that, with respect to landfills, it is not the land that is being utilized but rather the space above the land. According to the commentary, the space may be depreciable. Several cites to court cases are provided. Encouraged, Anna retrieves and carefully reads each court case. The court case *Sexton* is particularly on point with her client's fact pattern. As a final step, she checks the citator with respect to *Sexton* and finds that *Sexton* continues to be followed. Anna is ready to write her memorandum.

Sample Research Memorandum

To:	Dirtdigger, Inc.
From:	Anna Marie & Associates
Date:	July 5, 1997
Subject:	Landfill depreciation

FACTS Dirtdigger, Inc. began business in 1980 and is engaged in the collection and disposal of waste. Its current annual revenues are approximately $10,000,000. In order to expand, it acquires a new landfill outside Chicago. In 1997, Dirtdigger, Inc. paid $3,000,000 for 300 acres of real estate to be used as a landfill. Dirtdigger estimates that the salvage value of the landfill after it is closed will be $500,000.

ISSUE The tax issue is whether the purchase of the landfill is a depreciable asset.

APPLICABLE LAW AND ANALYSIS IRC Section 167(a) permits a deduction for the reasonable exhaustion, wear and tear, and obsolescence of property used in the taxpayer's trade or business. In this case, the taxpayer bought real estate to use as a landfill in its business. Land as such is not depreciable; however, several court cases have held that the space in, on, or above the land may constitute a property right that is separate from the land, and as such could qualify for depreciation under Section 167 (*John J. Sexton*, 42 TC 1094 [1964], *H. Kendrick Sanders* 75 TC 157 [1980], and *Browning-Ferris Industries, Inc.*, TC Memo 1987-147).

In *Sexton*, the U.S. Tax Court interpreted IRC Section 167(a) as permitting "a taxpayer to recover annually its capital investment in a wasting asset over the useful life of the asset in its business." As the space for dumping is exhausted, the usefulness of the property for business declines.

The only difference between the *Sexton* case and yours is that *Sexton* bought land that had a manmade excavation on it. In your case, the hollows and concavities are natural properties of the land. This difference is resolved in *H. Kendrick Sanders,* which has an identical fact pattern as that in the *Sexton* case except that *Sanders* did not buy land that had already been excavated. In the *Sanders* case, it is stated that there is no real difference attributable to the issue of whether the land was excavated or not, "air rights may be a separate property right from the land whether the property is flat or concave." Of primary importance is the fact that the property was purchased for use as a dump site in both of these cases.

It was concluded in both of the above cases as well as in a more recent case, *Browning-Ferris Industries, Inc.*, that the value of the depreciable interest is the difference between the value of the land prior to commencement of the dumping and the value of the land once it is no longer useful in the taxpayer's business. To apply this rule in your case, the depreciable interest would be $2.5 million ($3 million cost less $0.5 million salvage value.)

In the above cited cases, the units of production method of depreciation was deemed to be the proper method for calculating the annual deduction. In *Browning-Ferris Industries, Inc.*, the corporation sought approval for a particular landfill capacity and recorded the amount of waste that it dumped into the landfill. Because the corporation conducted annual surveys of the amount of space in the pit that was utilized each year in its garbage business, the Court allowed the corporation's depreciation calculations.

In your case, the annual depreciation deduction is equal to the total depreciable basis of $2.5 million multiplied by the percentage of total capacity filled each year. For example, if the landfill were filled to fifteen percent of its capacity in the first year of operations, the depreciation deduction would be $375,000 ($2.5 million x 15%) for the first year. Please note that the depreciation deduction must be taken in the same year as the corresponding space is exhausted or the deduction will be disallowed.

RECOMMENDATION Case law supports the deduction of depreciation for the landfill by the unit of production method. In your situation, a total of $2.5 million may be expensed over the useful life of the landfill. Each year's deduction should be computed based on the percentage of total capacity used. In case of an audit, you must be able to defend the salvage value estimate as reasonable and keep accurate records of the amount of waste dumped each year in order to avoid any problems with the deductibility of the purchase of the landfill.

SUMMARY

Tax research is legal research. If the tax accountant diligently follows the steps outlined in this chapter, he or she can develop a strong, defensible tax position for his or her client. The accountant should feel confident that the tax position taken will be sustained if challenged in a tax audit.

The following research cases are based on issues that may arise in the corporate income tax area. They were constructed assuming a minimal background in corporate tax law. Your job is to try to minimize taxes for your client in both a legal and professional manner. Assume facts occur during the current year unless otherwise specified.

Notes:

Exercise 7-5   **Name:** _____

Locating Tax Sources on the Internet **Section:** _____

Instructions: ***Locate each of the following on an Internet site. Specify the URL you utilized to locate the item.***

1. Form 1120   _____

2. IRS home page   _____

3. Your state tax home page   _____

Exercise 7-6   Name: _____

Applied Tax Research   Section: _____

Instructions: Using the following case information, complete the worksheet questions below.

The Occupational Safety and Health Administration (OSHA) requires companies with asbestos-insulated manufacturing equipment to perform costly procedures in connection with the use of and repairs to such equipment. As a result, your client concluded that replacing the asbestos with another (non-asbestos) thermal lining would be less expensive in the long run than complying with OSHA's procedures. Your client would like to know how the cost associated with purchasing the thermal linings should be treated for tax purposes.

Part 1. What is (are) the tax issue(s)?

_____

_____

_____

Part 2. Generate a list of keywords or IRC sections you would use to research this issue.

_____   _____

_____   _____

_____   _____

_____   _____

Part 3. Search the tax service database using the keywords and identify the relevant primary sources. (Do not cite the editorial explanations.)

Cite: _____   Cite: _____

Cite: _____   Cite: _____

Cite: _____   Cite: _____

Cite: _____   Cite: _____

Part 4. Prepare a memorandum documenting your recommendations for this situation. Be sure to use good form and check both spelling and grammar.

Part 5. Update your research using the database and a citator to make sure all primary sources you relied upon are still valid. Any current developments or changes need to be documented in your research memorandum.

Exercise 7-7　　　　　　　　　　　Name: _____

Applied Tax Research　　　　　　　Section: _____

Instructions: Using the following case information, complete the worksheet questions below.

This year your client established Videoland, Inc. He purchased $50,000 worth of videocassettes for the current year. He plans to rent these videos to the public and would like to know how the purchase price of the videos should be treated for tax purposes. Specify the years in which he may take a deduction.

Part 1. What is (are) the tax issue(s)?

_____

_____

_____

_____

Part 2. Generate a list of keywords or IRC sections you would use to research this issue.

_____　　　_____

_____　　　_____

_____　　　_____

_____　　　_____

Part 3. Search the tax service database using the keywords and identify the relevant primary sources. (Do not cite the editorial explanations.)

Cite: _____　　Cite: _____

Cite: _____　　Cite: _____

Cite: _____　　Cite: _____

Cite: _____　　Cite: _____

Part 4. Prepare a memorandum documenting your recommendations for this situation. Be sure to use good form and check both spelling and grammar.

Part 5. Update your research using the database and a citator to make sure all primary sources you relied upon are still valid. Any current developments or changes need to be documented in your research memorandum.

Exercise 7-8   Name: _____

Applied Tax Research   Section: _____

Instructions: Using the following case information, complete the worksheet questions below.

> Electric Illumination Corporation is a public utility company that uses coal to generate its power. It wishes to expand its business in another region by constructing a nuclear-based plant. The estimated time for building the plant is ten years at an approximate cost of $12,000,000 (which includes $2,000,000 for the land). In addition, thirty salaried employees would be paid a total of $1,000,000 to supervise the construction over the ten-year period. In the eleventh year before the actual operation of the nuclear plant would begin, Electric would have to spend an estimated $600,000 to train employees how to use the nuclear power facilities. Electric would like to know how each of these costs should be treated for tax purposes.

Part 1. What is (are) the tax issue(s)?

_____

_____

_____

_____

Part 2. Generate a list of keywords or IRC sections you would use to research this issue.

_____   _____

_____   _____

_____   _____

Part 3. Search the tax service database using the keywords and identify the relevant primary sources. (Do not cite the editorial explanations.)

Cite: _____   Cite: _____

Cite: _____   Cite: _____

Cite: _____   Cite: _____

Part 4. Prepare a memorandum documenting your recommendations for this situation. Be sure to use good form and check both spelling and grammar.

Part 5. Update your research using the database and a citator to make sure all primary sources you relied upon are still valid. Any current developments or changes need to be documented in your research memorandum.

Exercise 7-9

Name: _____

Applied Tax Research

Section: _____

Instructions: Using the following case information, complete the worksheet questions below.

Corporation X is a closely held corporation that uses the accrual method of accounting for tax purposes. Y and Z, husband and wife, each own fifty percent of the stock of Corporation X. Y and Z use the cash-basis method for filing their joint tax return.

On December 14, 1997, Corporation X accrues bonuses to Y and Z of $10,000 each. The bonuses are paid on January 20, 1998. All taxpayers operate on a calendar-year basis. Corporation X would like to know in which year it can deduct the bonuses.

Part 1. What is (are) the tax issue(s)?

_____

_____

_____

_____

Part 2. Generate a list of keywords or IRC sections you would use to research this issue.

_____   _____

_____   _____

_____   _____

Part 3. Search the tax service database using the keywords and identify the relevant primary sources. (Do not cite the editorial explanations.)

Cite: _____   Cite: _____

Cite: _____   Cite: _____

Cite: _____   Cite: _____

Part 4. Prepare a memorandum documenting your recommendations for this situation. Be sure to use good form and check both spelling and grammar.

Part 5. Update your research using the database and a citator to make sure all primary sources you relied upon are still valid. Any current developments or changes need to be documented in your research memorandum.

Exercise 7-10   Name: _____
Applied Tax Research   Section: _____

Instructions: Using the following case information, complete the worksheet questions below.

On September 1, 1997, Mac Corporation acquired the plant and equipment of a steel mill that had been idle for a period of time in order to expand its current steel mill operations. The purchase price was $15,000,000. As specified in the terms of the purchase agreement, the plant was in good working condition and operations could begin after a brief start-up period.

Mac incurred additional costs of $3,000,000 from the date of acquisition through 1998. Of the total additional expenditures of $3,000,000, Mac capitalized $600,000 relating to new equipment acquired and $300,000 as building improvements. Mac would like to know how the remaining $2,100,000 of expenditures should be treated for tax purposes. Most of these expenditures were incurred before operations of the new steel mill began.

Part 1. What is (are) the tax issue(s)?

_____

_____

_____

_____

Part 2. Generate a list of keywords or IRC sections you would use to research this issue.

_____   _____

_____   _____

_____   _____

Part 3. Search the tax service database using the keywords and identify the relevant primary sources. (Do not cite the editorial explanations.)

Cite: _____   Cite: _____

Cite: _____   Cite: _____

Cite: _____   Cite: _____

Part 4. Prepare a memorandum documenting your recommendations for this situation. Be sure to use good form and check both spelling and grammar.

Part 5. Update your research using the database and a citator to make sure all primary sources you relied upon are still valid.   Any current developments or changes need to be documented in your research memorandum.

Exercise 7-11   Name: _____

Applied Tax Research   Section: _____

Instructions: Using the following case information, complete the worksheet questions below.

Gasoil, Inc. owned a manufacturing plant that it built on land it had purchased. The land was not contaminated at the time of the purchase. The taxpayer's manufacturing operations discharged hazardous waste that was disposed of on the land.

Public outrage and environmental regulations pressured Gasoil to incur the following expenses during the current year: $1,500,000 for the safe removal of the contaminated soil, $500,000 to backfill the excavated areas with uncontaminated soil, and $5,000,000 for the construction of a groundwater treatment system. Gasoil would like to know how each of these expenditures should be treated for tax purposes.

Part 1. What is (are) the tax issue(s)?

_____

_____

_____

_____

Part 2. Generate a list of keywords or IRC sections you would use to research this issue.

_____   _____

_____   _____

_____   _____

Part 3. Search the tax service database using the keywords and identify the relevant primary sources. (Do not cite the editorial explanations.)

Cite: _____   Cite: _____

Cite: _____   Cite: _____

Cite: _____   Cite: _____

Part 4. Prepare a memorandum documenting your recommendations for this situation. Be sure to use good form and check both spelling and grammar.

Part 5. Update your research using the database and a citator to make sure all primary sources you relied upon are still valid. Any current developments or changes need to be documented in your research memorandum.

Exercise 7-12   Name: _____

Applied Tax Research   Section: _____

Instructions: Using the following case information, complete the worksheet questions below.

> Mega, Inc. purchased new computers and software totaling $300,000 during the current year. Mega would like to deduct this expense as quickly as possible for tax purposes. Advise Mega how this cost should be treated and be specific.

Part 1. What is (are) the tax issue(s)?

_____

_____

_____

_____

Part 2. Generate a list of keywords or IRC sections you would use to research this issue.

_____   _____

_____   _____

_____   _____

_____   _____

Part 3. Search the tax service database using the keywords and identify the relevant primary sources. (Do not cite the editorial explanations.)

Cite: _____   Cite: _____

Cite: _____   Cite: _____

Cite: _____   Cite: _____

Cite: _____   Cite: _____

Part 4. Prepare a memorandum documenting your recommendations for this situation. Be sure to use good form and check both spelling and grammar.

Part 5. Update your research using the database and a citator to make sure all primary sources you relied upon are still valid.   Any current developments or changes need to be documented in your research memorandum.

Exercise 7-13
Applied Tax Research

Name: _____

Section: _____

Instructions: Using the following case information, complete the worksheet questions below.

Joe Taxpayer purchased shares of IBM stock at different time intervals. His purchases were as follows:			
	Date	Shares	Amount
Previous Year:	Jan 11	210	$2,000
Current Year:	Feb 11	220	$2,000
	Mar 15	230	$2,000
	Apr 19	230	$2,000

On July 15 of the current year, Joe sold 400 shares for $4,000. Joe would like to know how much income (gain) he should report from this sale.

Part 1. What is (are) the tax issue(s)?

_____

_____

_____

_____

Part 2. Generate a list of keywords or IRC sections you would use to research this issue.

_____   _____

_____   _____

_____   _____

_____   _____

continued on back

Part 3. Search the tax service database using the keywords and identify the relevant primary sources. (Do not cite the editorial explanations.)

Cite: _____   Cite: _____

Cite: _____   Cite: _____

Cite: _____   Cite: _____

Cite: _____   Cite: _____

Part 4. Prepare a memorandum documenting your recommendations for this situation. Be sure to use good form and check both spelling and grammar.

Part 5. Update your research using the database and a citator to make sure all primary sources you relied upon are still valid.   Any current developments or changes need to be documented in your research memorandum.

Chapter 8
Advanced Internet Tools

INTRODUCTION

Chapter 2 provided you with basic Internet tools and techniques. The purpose of this chapter is to increase your technical proficiency by providing an overview of the Internet environment, a vocabulary of terms often encountered, and an introduction to additional tools and techniques that enhance information sharing and collaborative work.

THE INTERNET

DARPA (Defense Advanced Research Projects Agency) began work toward an Internet technology in the mid-1970s. The DARPA technology includes a set of network standards that specify how computers communicate, as well as a set of conventions for interconnecting networks and routing network traffic. Officially named the TCP/IP Internet Protocol Suite and commonly called TCP/IP (Transmission Control Protocol/Internet Protocol), the suite of protocols can be used to communicate across any set of interconnected networks. For example, some corporations use TCP/IP to interconnect all networks within their corporation, although the corporation has no connection to outside networks. Other groups use TCP/IP for communication among geographically distant sites.

Although the TCP/IP technology by itself is interesting, it is particularly important because its success has been demonstrated on a large scale. It forms the base for a large network that connects most major research institutions, including university, corporate, and government labs. The National Science Foundation (NSF), the Department of Energy (DOE), the Department of Defense (DOD), the Health and Human Services Agency (HHS), and the National Aeronautics and Space Administration (NASA) all participate, using TCP/IP to connect many of their research sites with those of DARPA. The result is an entity, known as the connected Internet, the DARPA/NSF Internet, the TCP/IP Internet, or for most of us the Internet. The Internet allows researchers, educators, students, and other professionals at connected institutions to share information with colleagues across the country as easily as they share it with individuals in the next room.

The Internet is now a public, self-sustaining facility accessible to more than thirty million people worldwide. Apart from "surfing" the Internet, e-mail is probably the most widely used application on the Internet. Today's Internet is a vast storehouse of information. According to *Wired* (March 1997), there are more than 150 million Web sites.

IP Addresses

As part of your research you will be accessing information at various sites on the Internet. Where you are on the Internet and where you might want to go is defined by an IP address. An IP address represents a location on the Internet where information is stored. Familiarity with IP addresses, what they represent, and where they take you will make your research project much easier.

Consider the Internet a large network like the one that operates at your university or firm. The difference of course is that the Internet represents a virtual network structure as opposed to a physical structure. Designers of the Internet made it independent of the hardware configuration of any single user. So, concerns about sharing information created on a Macintosh with users operating in other environments (Unix, Windows, O/S2) do not exist. To create addresses on the Internet the designers chose a scheme that is analogous to the physical network addressing at your university or firm. Each host machine is assigned an integer address called its Internet address or IP address.

The Internet addressing was chosen to make information packet routing across the network efficient. Each host is assigned a unique 32-bit Internet address used to communicate with that host. The IP address is a series of numbers that describe a connection to the Internet not the actual machine connected. Although the Internet address is a 32-bit binary representation of the address (i.e., 0's and 1's), an IP address you see would look like this: 128.248.208.57.
Each number separated by the decimal point represents one byte. In binary this same number would look like this: 10000000 11001100 11010000 00111001.

Thus, you see "128.248.208.57" and your computer sees "10000000 11001100 11010000 00111001." Each address contains two pieces of information: network id (netid) and host id (hostid). The "Netid" is the actual unique network address. Hosts (such as PCs, file servers, and routers) are connected to networks and have a "Hostid." These two numbers make up the 32-bit IP address.

IP addresses are the means by which computers on a network communicate. A computer's use of an IP address is analogous to phone numbers or street addresses. Thus, when "surfing" the net via your Web browser, the Web browser seeks information at various IP addresses provided by links imbedded in the Web pages that you observe.

More often than not you will encounter information at addresses that look like the following:

        www.adobe.com   or   thomas.loc.gov   or   www.uic.edu

How do these addresses relate to the IP addresses we discussed earlier and what do the names mean for purposes of conducting a research project? These names are associated with an IP address through a hierarchical naming system called the Domain Name System (DNS). It is important not to confuse this DNS with the DNS (Domain Name Server) provided in the vocabulary list.

Domain Name System

The Domain Name System (DNS) was the replacement system to the original ARPANET hosts.txt mechanism. The DNS is similar to the system that determines your phone number. An area code, exchange, and subscriber number determine your phone number and, depending on the caller's location, the area code may or may not be used to make a connection. We read the hierarchy for the phone number system from left to right. Thus, area code is the top-level authority followed by exchange and subscriber number. In the DNS system we read the hierarchy from right to left. For example, consider the following fictional address:

actg.cba.univname.edu.us

Reading from right to left, we can determine that the site is in the United States (*us*), at an educational institution (*edu*), that is a university (*univname*), in the College of Business Administration (*cba*), and in the Department of Accounting (*actg*). The first letter set (us) is not commonly used for sites in the United States.

The Internet Authority controls the designations of country (*us*) and the five generic domains (*edu*) (ISO, "Codes for the Representation of Names of Countries," ISO-3166, International Standards Organization, May 1981). The university must request registration for its university address with the Internet Authority (*edu*) but has the authority to assign lower-level names (*cba* and *actg*).

At the formation of the Domain Name System (DNS) in the mid-1980s, the Internet was still primarily a U.S. academic and research network. As the Internet began to grow internationally, many countries set up domain hierarchies based on the geographic country code, despite traditional categorical top-level domains being available to all. In the United States, most hosts continued to use the traditional top-level domains, instead of the geographical "US" domain. The controlling organization for domain names is located at INTERNIC.NET.

The top-level structure of names used by DNS contains five worldwide generic domains ("COM", "EDU", "NET", "ORG", and "INT"), two U.S.-only generic domains ("MIL" and "GOV"), and country code domains (e.g., "US" for the United States, "AU" for Australia, etc.) the highest naming authority (domain). Within the U.S. domain, the domain name structure has been extended to include counties, cities, K–12 institutions and other organizations with Internet connections.

General Domains

Com. This domain is intended for commercial entities. Registration of corporate sites in this domain make searching for company information quite easy. Companies with internet connections generally follow a naming convention like: www.CompanyName.COM. Thus, if you were interested in finding information about Dell Corporation, you could type the following address for your Web browser to access: http://www.dell.com. The http:// is provided because it is the proper addressing scheme for accessing information via a Web browser. If other information acquisition tools are being used (i.e., Telnet or FTP, to be discussed later) the appropriate address would be www.dell.com. However, a computer acting as a server for one of these information retrieval methods must exist at the organization site.

Edu. This domain was originally intended for all educational institutions. Many universities, colleges, schools, educational service organizations, and educational consortia have registered here. Recently a decision to limit further registrations to four-year colleges and universities was made. Schools and two-year colleges will be registered in the country domains. If you are interested in information about a university other than your own but are not sure of the address, try: www.UniversityInitials.EDU or www.UniversityName.EDU. Thus, if you wanted to know something about DePaul University, you would provide the following address to your Web browser: http://www.depaul.EDU.

Net. This domain is intended to hold only network provider computers; that is, the NIC and NOC computers, the administrative computers, and the network node computers. The network provider customers would have their own domain names (not in the NET top-level domain).

Org. This domain is intended as the miscellaneous top-level domain for organizations that did not fit anywhere else. For example, The Tax Analysts, a tax group responsible for the publication *Tax Notes,* can be contacted at http://www.tax.org.

Int. This domain is for organizations established by international treaties or international databases. For example, the address for the European Union is: http://europa.eu.int/.

U.S.-Only Generic Domains

Gov. This domain was originally intended for any kind of government office or agency. More recently a decision was made to register only agencies of the U.S. Federal government in this domain. State and local agencies are registered in the country domains (see US Domain, below). The U.S. Census Bureau resides at http://www.census.gov/.

Mil. This domain is used by the U.S. military. Wright Patterson Air Force Base in Ohio has the following address: http://www.wpafb.af.mil/.

Country Code Domains

US. As an example of a country domain, the US domain provides for the registration of all kinds of entities in the United States based on political geography, that is, a hierarchy of <entity-name>. <locality>.<state-code>.US. Branches of the US domain are provided within each state for schools (K12), community colleges (CC), technical schools (TEC), state government agencies (STATE), councils of governments (COG), libraries (LIB), museums (MUS), and several other generic types of entities. For example, the Houston Museum of Natural Science is located at http://www.hmns.mus.tx.us.

This concludes the discussion of the Internet, IP addresses, and Domains. Continuing review of the information presented here using various Internet resources will develop and improve your technical competency. Knowledge in this area, in coordination with competent search engine use, should enhance your ability to use Internet resources for applied professional research.

Exercise 8-1   Name: _____

Obtaining Information   Section: _____

from Education Sites

Instructions: Complete each of the following by accessing the information using Internet resources. Provide the address you used to access the information.

What is the domain name for your university? _____

Does your university have a home page? _____

Source address: _____

What information is provided on your university's home page?

_____

_____

_____

_____

_____

Locate another university's home page.

Source address: _____

What information is provided on that university's home page?

_____

_____

_____

_____

_____

Exercise 8-2
Locating Information
from Accounting Firms

Name: _____

Section: _____

Instructions: Complete each of the following by accessing the information using Internet resources. Provide the address you used to access the information.

Find the home pages for three of the largest public accounting firms.

Source address: _____

Source address: _____

Source address: _____

What sorts of information are available on these home pages, and what can you learn about these firms from this information?

_____

_____

_____

_____

_____

_____

_____

VOCABULARY

One thing that makes us uncomfortable in a new environment is the terminology. Many of you may already be "Web surfers," with a rudimentary vocabulary already in place. However, surfing the Web and being a competent applied researcher using the Internet is different.

As future accountants, applied research using the Internet will be but one function of your job as an information broker. You may also be called upon to give instruction to clients or colleagues about accessing information, advice about how that information should be presented, or attest to the validity of information presented at an Internet site.

The starting point for this level of technical competency is increasing your vocabulary specific to the Internet environment. Below is a list of vocabulary words along with their definitions. Being comfortable with these terms before continuing in this chapter will be helpful for you.

ASCII. The most common format for text files in computers and on the Internet. Files sent over the Internet must be converted to ASCII before they can be sent. In an ASCII file, each alphabetic, numeric, or special character is represented with a 7-bit binary number (a string of seven 0s or 1s). In all, 128 possible characters are defined. The American National Standards Institute (ANSI) developed ASCII.

Bookmark. When using a Web browser, a bookmark is a link to a Web site that has been added to a list of saved links. When you are looking at a particular Web site or home page and want to be able to quickly get back to it in a future session, you can create a bookmark for it. Netscape and some other browsers use the bookmark idea. Microsoft's Internet Explorer uses the term *favorite*.

Browser. A browser is a program that provides a way to look at, read, and even hear information on the Internet. A Web browser is a client program that uses the Hypertext Transport Control Protocol (HTTP) to request information from Web servers located on the Internet. Currently, the most popular browsers are Netscape Navigator and Microsoft's Internet Explorer.

Cache. A cache (pronounced CASH) is a place to store something temporarily. Web pages viewed in the browser window are stored in the browser's cache directory located on your hard disk. This allows the page to be viewed later without requesting the original information from the server again.

Chatting. Chatting is talking on the Internet in real-time. Usually, this "talking" is the exchange of typed-in messages requiring one site as the repository for the messages (or "chat site") and a group of users who take part from anywhere on the Internet. However, a chat can occur between collaborators who each have the proper software.

Client. A client is the program or user requesting an action or information in a client/server relationship. For example, you and your Web browser are the client requesting information from Web sites on the Internet.

Database. A database is a collection of data organized so that we can easily access its contents, managed, and updated. A relational database is one in which data are defined so that they can be reorganized and accessed in many different ways. A distributed database is one that can be dispersed or replicated among different points in a network. An object-oriented database is one that is congruent with the data defined in object classes and subclasses. Usually, databases represent large aggregations of data records or files, such as sales transactions or product profiles. Typically, a database manager provides users the capabilities of controlling read/write access, specifying report generation, and analyzing usage.

Domain. In computing and telecommunication in general, a domain is a set of owned knowledge identified by a name. Typically, the knowledge is a collection of facts about some program entities or a number of network points or addresses. On the Internet, domains are network address sets. Domains are organized in levels, the top level being geographic or purpose. The second level identifies a unique place within the top-level domain and is, in fact, equivalent to a unique address on the Internet (or IP). Lower levels of domain may also be used.

E-mail (Electronic Mail). The exchange of computer-stored messages by telecommunication. Messages are encoded in ASCII text. However, you can also send nontext files, such as graphic images and sound files, as attachments sent in binary streams. E-mail was one of the first uses of the Internet and is still the most popular single use.

Extranet. An extranet is a collaborative network that uses Internet technology to link businesses with their suppliers, customers, or other businesses that share common goals. An extranet is likely to be a part of the firm's intranet made accessible to other firms. The shared information is usually accessible only to the collaborating parties or clients.

Gateway. A gateway is an Internet site that provides access to specialized information. For example, there are accounting information gateways, tax information gateways, and state, local, and federal government information gateways. Because these specialized Web sites exist for various information topics, your information search time can be radically reduced.

GIF. A graphics file that is an image formatted according to Graphics Interchange Format (GIF). The newest format GIF89s allows a set of images to be combined into what we call an animated GIF. The animated GIF is constructed much like an animated cartoon. Images of the object at various stages of change are sequenced and timed to give the feeling of continuous action.

Groupware. Groupware refers to software that supports people working together in a collective effort but who are geographically dispersed. Groupware services can include the sharing of calendars, collective writing, e-mail handling, shared database access, electronic meetings with each person able to see and display information to others, and other activities.

Helper Application. In Netscape and other Web browsers, a helper application is a program that can handle a specific kind of file, which is indicated in the file transmission header by its MIME type or in storage by its file name extension. A few helper applications, such as those that handle HTML, GIF, and JPEG files, come with the browser. The user can download and add additional ones to the browser. Other than those that come with the browser, helper applications are usually run in a separate window (unlike plug-in applications, which are integrated with the main browser program).

Home Page. A home page is the first page presented at a Web site or presence on the Internet. The usual address for a Web site is the home page address, although you can enter the address (URL) of any page and have that page sent to you.

HTML. HTML is the set of "markup" symbols or codes inserted in a file intended for display on a Web browser. The markup tells the Web browser how to display the information for the user. HTML is defined both by a standards committee and by proprietary extenders of the language such as Netscape and Microsoft.

HTTP. The hypertext transfer protocol (HTTP) is the set of rules for exchanging files (text, graphic images, sound, video, and other multimedia files) on the Internet. HTTP is an application protocol for requesting and sending information. The essential idea that underlies HTTP is the idea that files can contain references to other files whose selection will elicit additional information transfer requests. Every Web server, in addition to the Web files it can transmit to clients, contains an HTTP daemon, a program that handles HTTP information requests. A Web browser is an HTTP client, sending requests to HTTP server daemons. When the browser user requests a file either by "opening" a Web file (typing in a Uniform Resource Locator or URL) or clicking on a hypertext link, the browser builds an HTTP request and sends it to the Internet Protocol (IP) address indicated by the URL. The standard HTTP request for information takes the following form: http://InternetSite/FileRequested.

Intranet. An intranet is a network that is contained within an enterprise. It usually consists of many interlinked local area networks that may or may not include a connection to the outside Internet. The main purpose of an intranet is usually to share company information and computing resources among employees. Accounting firms and corporations are some of the most innovative users of intranets and your daily activity, continuing education, and collaboration with peers and superiors will likely involve considerable use of an intranet.

List Server. A list server is a program that handles subscription requests for a mailing list and distributes new messages from the list's members to the entire list of subscribers as they occur. For example, the Government Accounting Office (GAO) has several list servers that update subscribers about new GAO reports and decisions on government contract disputes. A daily e-mail message is transmitted to all subscribers.

Plug-in. Plug-in applications are programs that can be used as part of your Web browser. Plug-ins were developed as applications that, when installed, become an integral part of the browser's functions. Adobe Acrobat Reader is a popular viewer program for pdf (portable document files) that operates as a plug-in and allows the pdf image file to be viewed and printed from the browser window.

POP3 (Post Office Protocol 3). POP3 is a client-server protocol with which e-mail is received and held. Messages held at the Internet server are accessed using a specific e-mail software package (Eudora, Internet Mail, Netscape) or using an interface program provided by the Internet server (Pine, RICEmail).

PPP (Point-to-Point Protocol). PPP is a TCP/IP protocol used for communication between two machines that are configured for communication with each other (thus, point-to-point). PPP is usually preferred to the Serial Line Internet Protocol (SLIP) because it can handle synchronous as well as asynchronous communication. PPP can share a line with other users and it has error detection that SLIP lacks.

Protocol. In Internet and computer vernacular, a protocol is the special set of rules of communication that the terminals or nodes (and related software) in a telecommunication connection use when they send signals back and forth. Protocols exist at several levels in a telecommunication connection. On the Internet, there are the TCP/IP protocols, consisting of: (1) TCP (Transport Control Protocol), which uses a set of rules to exchange messages with other Internet points at the information packet level; (2) IP (Internet Protocol), which uses a set of rules to send and receive messages at the Internet address level.

Server. In the Web context, a server is a computer connected to the Internet, "serving" Web pages to people who request them. A server is usually a larger computer "serving" a set of smaller computers (workstations) that are clients. However, sometimes the same computer will act as a client or a server, depending on the operation requested. A Web server is the computer serving requested HTML pages or files. A Web client is the computer associated with the user. The Web browser on your computer is client software that requests HTML files from Web servers.

SGML (Standard Generalized Markup Language). SGML is a standard for how to specify a document markup language or tag set. The specification itself is called a document-type definition (DTD). SGML is based on the idea that documents have structural and other semantic elements that we can describe without reference to how such elements should be displayed. The actual display of such a document may vary, depending on the output medium and style preferences. HTML is a subset of SGML. The Security and Exchange Commission's database of electronically filed annual reports (Edgar) stores documents using SGML. The SEC provides a converter that converts the SGML to WordPerfect format.

SLIP (Serial Line Internet Protocol). SLIP is a TCP/IP protocol used for communication between two machines that are previously configured for communication with each other.

SMTP (Simple Mail Transfer Protocol). SMTP is a TCP/IP protocol governing electronic mail transmission and reception. POP3 determines how your mail is handled once you receive a message (held at a server or downloaded locally). SMTP determines how mail messages are sent and received. It defines how the e-mail message is encoded, addressed, and delivered.

TCP/IP (Transmission Control Protocol/Internet Protocol). TCP/IP is the program that every Internet user and every Internet information server runs. Although TCP and IP are the most important, TCP/IP is really a suite of protocols. The ones you are most likely to use (directly or indirectly) are HTTP, FTP, Telnet, Gopher, PPP, and SMTP.

URL. A URL is the address of a Web page. A URL (uniform resource locator) is the unique Internet address of a single HTML page or file. The address includes a domain name (which is actually a unique Internet server address) and a hierarchical description of a file location on the server. An example would look like the following: actg.cba.univname.edu/classes/actg/actg501/syllabus.html. To access this URL, the proper HTTP protocol would be added to complete the address.

WAIS (Wide-Area Information Servers or Service). Wide-area information servers (WAIS) are an Internet system in which specialized subject databases are created at multiple server locations, kept track of by a directory of servers at one location, and made accessible for searching by users with WAIS client programs. The user of WAIS is provided with or obtains a list of distributed databases. The user enters a search argument for a selected database and the client then accesses all the servers on which the database is distributed. The results describe each text that meets the search requirements. The user can then retrieve the full text. For example, you can search for a book at any library in a state school library system using a WAIS. WAIS is pronounced "ways" and uses its own Internet protocol, an extension of (Information Retrieval Service Definition and Protocol Specification for Library Applications) of the National Information Standards Organization.

Web Site or Website. A Web site (or Website) is a collection of information files on the Web that includes a beginning file called a home page. From the home page, you can access all other pages on the site. Web site is sometimes confused with "Web server." Earlier we noted that a server is a computer that holds the files for one or more sites. A very large Web site may reside on several servers in many different geographic places.

This concludes the vocabulary list of general Internet terminology that will be useful as you become proficient with the Internet. This list should extend the vocabulary you already know and cover many terms you will initially encounter on the Internet.

COLLABORATIVE RESEARCH TOOLS AND TECHNIQUES

The original Internet developers were scientists on opposite coasts and researchers at the Department of Defense who needed an effective way to communicate and transmit data between research centers. Their objective in developing an Internet was to enhance the collaboration between research teams housed at geographically dispersed locations without concern for the platform or operating system used and the time and travel costs.

Although we might think of geographic dispersion as being in different states or countries, it might also be different suburbs in the same metropolitan area or dorms at the same college or university. As more classes require team or cooperative projects, software that reduces scheduling problems and allows effective information sharing becomes increasingly necessary.

Synchronous and Asynchronous Activity

We can categorize information transmission and collaboration with colleagues as one of two modes–synchronous or asynchronous. Synchronous mode is having collaborators physically present with interactive information flow. This mode has positive benefits that include real-time information transmission and error correction, and secured data exchange. Although many of us would prefer to operate in "synchronous mode," scheduling everyone to be in the same place simultaneously can be frustrating at best.

Asynchronous mode is when collaborators are not physically present and information transmission and data exchange are delayed. Collaboration in this mode occurs over a much longer period and task completion may not require the physical presence of the collaborator.

Enhanced Asynchronous and Synchronous Interaction using Technology

Past technology developments included means to reduce synchronous and asynchronous interaction costs. Relatively recent developments include facsimile (FAX) machines, voice mail, answering machines, and other types of asynchronous interaction. The primary problem with these asynchronous methods is the limit on the type of information transmitted. Efforts to enhance synchronous information transmissions include conference calls and video conferencing.

Recent advances in Internet technology are directed at providing cost-effective collaboration and information transmission. Improvements provide for more effective asynchronous interaction and virtual synchronous interaction.

Asynchronous Improvements

E-mail is one of the most underutilized forms of asynchronous interaction. Individuals who have recently discovered e-mail find it a means of communicating that is cost-effective and efficient for transmitting information that does not require synchronous interaction. What many individuals are not aware of are the data transmission options available through the "attach file" or "attachment" feature of e-mail software. Almost every Internet service provider (ISP) provides e-mail software capable of sending attachments.

Attachments

Most e-mail software packages allow the sender to include, as part of the e-mail transmission, an additional file containing information in a format not supported directly by the e-mail package. The process of attaching one of these files involves selecting the new message option from the appropriate pull-down menu and selecting the option to attach a file. After the "attach file" option has been selected, a dialog box asking the sender to select the file to attach will appear. After the sender selects the appropriate directory and file, a line appears as part of the e-mail header giving the address of the file being included as part of the e-mail message. The sender has the option of providing additional information or instructions in the body of the e-mail message before sending. When complete, the e-mail message is sent to the recipient like any other e-mail message.

The beauty of this option is that we can attach any file, whatever type, to an e-mail message. Thus, spreadsheets, word processor files, pictures, scanned documents, or any file that can be converted to an electronic format can be attached. If users are concerned about security or document manipulation, portable document files (pdf) using Adobe Exchange 3.0 (http://www.adobe.com/prodindex/acrobat/main.html) can be password protected and/or print restricted and attached to an e-mail message. We can attach multiple files to one e-mail message. To attach multiple files, repeat the process for attaching a single file for as many files that need to be attached.

For most users the process of file attachment is seamless and the manner in which the file is attached invisible. When we receive a message with an attachment, an icon showing the filename and type of file attached is found in the body of the e-mail message at the bottom (alternatively a text line indicating the name and original address [directory] of the file attached). To open the attached file the recipient needs only double click (left mouse button for Windows users) on the filename or icon. The necessary application software automatically opens the file for viewing or the recipient is prompted to indicate the software to be used.

The process, although simple, has the occasional problem. However, a few hints about how these problems arise and suggestions about avoiding these problems should make this a genuinely cost-effective means of transmitting data for most users. The problems encountered usually arise because of file size, encoding and decoding attached files, and different software preferences between sender and receiver.

Size. The problem with size is not one that the individual user can correct (except to the extent that attention is paid to the size of file sent). The file size parameter depends on the user's ISP and the ISP's software for handling e-mail. Size limits, however, are usually quite generous. For some systems, file size allowed, as an attachment, is as large as two to three megabytes. Such a file size would encompass small executable programs (.exe). Most word processor files are much smaller. For example, a five-page double-spaced file in Microsoft Word ranges from thirty to fifty KB depending on the formatting used. Thus, a file forty times that size could be attached to an e-mail message where the system allowed attachments as large as 2 megabytes. An awareness of the ISP's system constraint (when in doubt, ask) and the file size you are attempting to send will reduce this type of problem.

Encoding and Decoding. The invisible part of the attachment process is the encoding and decoding of the attached file. Sending files over the Internet requires that the file be converted to ASCII (American Standard Code for Information Interchange). Actually, application programs store files with both ASCII and binary coding. The coding that represents the text you have typed is ASCII. The coding that determines the formatting of your text is binary. The codes are stored together so that the document can be re-created when opened by the word processor.

To send a file as an attachment it must be converted to its ASCII character representation. There are three such conversion schemes found on the Internet. These are UUENCODE, BINHEX, and MIME. UUENCODE (Unix to Unix Encoding) is a popular conversion process for Unix and DOS/Windows platforms. BINHEX (*BIN*ARY *HEX*ADECIMAL) is another method for converting non-text files to ASCII and is popular on the Macintosh platform. MIME (Multipurpose Internet Mail Extensions) is considered the standard for attaching non-text files to standard Internet mail messages. Non-text files include graphics, spreadsheets, formatted word processor documents, sound files, and so on. An -mail program is said to be MIME compliant if it can both send and receive files using the MIME standard.

Problems arise when a file attached to an e-mail message is encoded using one scheme (your e-mail software does this automatically) to a user on a system set up to accept and translate one of the other schemes. The result of this mismatch will be an e-mail message that contains unintelligible characters as the body of the e-mail message received.

This problem can be avoided by knowing the default encoding scheme used by your e-mail software and that of the intended recipient. If a mismatch exists, three options are available. (1) Choose additional encoding software to encode the file before sending. However, this option requires additional effort and expense that might not be worthwhile. (2) Many e-mail packages allow the sender to choose the encoding scheme. For example, Eudora Pro 3.0 (http://www.eudora.com/) allows the user to select MIME, UUENCODE, or BINHEX as the encoding scheme for attachments. Thus, for known mismatches the encoding scheme can be changed to accommodate the recipient's encoding scheme. Finally, lobbying one's ISP for MIME-compliant e-mail software will make the process easier for all concerned.

Application Preferences. Many initiatives to share information electronically are stalled because collaborators or clients use different software for word processing or spreadsheet development. Neither of the previous problems discussed have a bearing on this problem.

Users simply prefer a particular application and are reluctant to change. However, this should not impede sharing information electronically. Most applications allow for file conversion both to and from other application programs. Under the Save As menu the selections are numerous. The key to avoiding problems is determining which selection represents the easiest conversion for the recipient. For example, in Word and WordPerfect a selection is provided to save the file with the ".doc" extension. When this extension is used, the information sharing between users of each of these applications is virtually error free.

The extension is not always necessary if the application of the sender and receiver are the same. However, we can reduce problems with opening attachments if we include the extension. Windows-based programs tend to assign a three-letter extension automatically. This is not true in the Macintosh world.

If the document to be sent does not contain much proprietary coding (e.g., equations, tables), a file type common to all word processors is Rich Text Format (rtf). This allows any word processor to send a primarily text-based document to any other word processor on any operating system. The file should contain as its extension either ".rtf" or ".doc". If you are unsure of the system used by the recipient, the ".doc" extension will have the fewest problems.

Finally, Microsoft has introduced application files called "viewers." There is a viewer application for each of the Microsoft applications and they are free from Microsoft (http://www.microsoft.com/msdownload/default.asp#viewers). A viewer is a restricted form of the Microsoft application with which it is associated. The viewers allow non-Microsoft product users to view and/or print but not change any Microsoft document with the appropriate viewer.

Attention to the problems discussed above can make asynchronous information transfers cost-effective and for the most part no more complicated than sending a fax. Recent technology changes allow e-mail attachments to make dramatic changes in how teams can exchange information.

Virtual Synchronicity

Multitudes of researchers at various research institutions are looking at the effects of synchronous interaction through the computer. As this research continues, many software packages are likely to appear as commercial offerings in the future. However, there is user-friendly synchronous interactive software available today. Lotus Notes is a software suite offering a substantial amount of synchronous interaction. However, much of the versatility of Lotus Notes is confined to users of Lotus' proprietary software. Novell's entry is called GroupWise and is available to users on Novell network systems. You may have Lotus Notes or GroupWise available at your institution. However, alternatives that do not require specific NetWare or network systems are available.

Two competitors offer synchronous capabilities for non-network-based interaction. The first is Microsoft's NetMeeting 2.0 (http://www.microsoft.com/netmeeting/), a Windows-based system (i.e., Windows 95, Windows NT). The second, Netscape Communicator 4.0 (Professional Edition Review http://www.netscape.com/inf/comprod/products/communicator/index.html), is a multiple platform system (i.e., Unix, Power Macintosh, OS/2, Windows 3.x, Windows 95,

Windows NT). Both packages have been tested on LANs, ISDN lines, and through dial-up facilities using a 28.8 modem. The features, albeit slower, are fully functional even through the 28.8 modem connection.

When individuals collaborate using this software it is often called conferencing and a conference can include up to fifty members. The purpose of collaborative software suites (as we refer to these packages) is to provide user interaction capabilities similar to face-to-face synchronous meetings without the simultaneous physical presence. Thus, the software provides a means for group members to talk to each other, share applications, share files, see one another, and in some cases search the Web together.

If everyone engaging in this collaboration form had the best and most capable hardware, conference members could interact with full video and audio capabilities that would allow multiple screen interactions. Unfortunately, the software, while almost, is not quite there. However, the greatest problem is usually the hardware configuration sitting on your desk or your collaborator's desk. Each package provides for interaction that fits the participant's hardware configuration.

These two software packages contain many similar attributes and as such the discussion will focus on these attributes rather than on the specific software package. When appropriate specific features are associated with the application. Some of these features include the following.

Chat. Using the Chat function, typed text messages become a part of the collaborative process. Chat also provides communication without audio support hardware. The Chat function has a "whisper" feature (NetMeeting 2.0) that lets you have a separate, private conversation with another person during a group chat session.

Whiteboard. A whiteboard program is a multi-page, multi-user-drawing application that enables users to sketch diagrams, organization charts, or share other graphic files. Whiteboards are object-oriented (versus pixel-oriented) and allow users to move and manipulate contents by clicking and dragging with a mouse. In addition, users can highlight or use remote pointers to point out specific content or sections of a shared page. Users' marks on the Whiteboard are identified by colors assigned when entering the conference.

Shared clipboard. The shared clipboard allows users to exchange information from a local document using cut, copy, and paste operations. Once the information is located on the clipboard, it can be pasted to a shared application (NetMeeting 2.0) used as part of group collaboration.

File transfer. File transfer allows file sending in the background to one or all current conference members. When files are sent to multiple conference members, each member can accept or decline the receipt. The file transfer occurs in the background as everyone continues sharing an application, using the whiteboard, or chatting.

Application sharing. In NetMeeting 2.0 (but not Netscape Communicator 4.0) conference members can share a program running on one computer. Users can review the same data or information, and see the actions as the person sharing the application works on the program (e.g., editing content or scrolling through information.) Participants can share Windows-based applications without any special knowledge of the application capabilities. The person sharing the application can choose to collaborate with other people in a call, and they can take turns editing or controlling the application. Only the user sharing the program needs to have the given application installed on her or his computer.

Video conferencing. With NetMeeting 2.0, users can send and receive real-time visual images with another conference member using any video for Windows-compatible equipment. Information can be exchanged face-to-face, and the camera can be used instantly to provide a view of objects being discussed. Combined with the audio and data capabilities of NetMeeting 2.0, you can both see and hear the other person, as well as share information and applications. We expect multiple video and audio connections in the near future. Currently Netscape Communicator 4.0 has no video capabilities but they are expected in the final release.

Each package contains additional features you should explore on your own. The features available make limits on the package uses a function of your imagination. These software packages give you a powerful and effective means of conducting a virtual synchronous interaction. You should expect to see this type of software as standard part of every desktop system in the future.

No matter what your primary interaction mode is; the technological tools described above should make that interaction more effective. There may be only one obstacle to using these improvements. That obstacle is a lack of information about what is available.

Exercise 8-3   **Name:** _____
Internet Terminology   **Section:** _____

*Instructions: Using an Internet browser, search for information to answer the following
questions. Be sure to provide the address where the information was located.*

1. Write a short answer explaining what a daemon is. Be sure to indicate how the word should
be pronounced.

_____

_____

_____

Source address: _____

2. Write a short description explaining the term *BITNET*.

_____

_____

Source address: _____

3. The Internet is sometimes referred to as cyberspace. Find a definition of *cyberspace* and
determine (if you can) where the term originated.

_____

_____

Source address: _____

4. Write a short explanation of the term *DIMM*.

_____

_____

Source address: _____

Exercise 8-4   Name: _____
Using Internet Applications   Section: _____

Instructions: Complete each of the following by accessing the information using Internet resources. Provide the address you used to access the information.

Netscape provides all users with a separate application called CoolTalk. What is CoolTalk and what conferencing ability does it have?

_____

_____

_____

Provide a description of an application referred to as POWWOW.

_____

_____

_____

Where can you find it and what capabilities does it provide?

_____

_____

_____

_____

Microsoft's conferencing software NetMeeting depends on ULS. What is ULS and how does it work?

_____

_____

Exercise 8-5 Name: _____
Using E-mail Section: _____

Send an e-mail message to a member of your class. What e-mail system does your school use?

_____

Does it have the option to send attachments? _____

Send an attachment to a member of your class. Did the attachment arrive safely? _____

If not, speculate what the problem might be. If the attachment arrived correctly, indicate the type of file you sent.

_____

_____

Determine the server that acts as your POP3 and SMTP server. _____

If you cannot, what do you believe were the roadblocks?

_____

_____

_____

Chapter 9
Financial Accounting
and Reporting Cases

INTRODUCTION

We intend the following cases to provide practice in applied professional research in accounting. The topics of the cases have been chosen to correspond to the content of chapters in many popular intermediate accounting textbooks.

These cases are intended to be simple with the focus on practicing the applied research process. Most of the cases have definitive authoritative literature passages. The applicable literature can be found using the applied research tools you have already learned.

Assume that all amounts are material.

CONCEPTUAL FRAMEWORK

Case CF-1

Sweet's Garages, Incorporated manufactures, delivers, and installs prefabricated garages and carports. All orders are manufactured on a custom basis and are shipped immediately upon completion of the manufacturing to the customer's location for installation. Since all orders are prepaid, Sweet's recognizes the sale upon completion of the manufacturing process. However, actual installation may occur up to four months later, depending upon the weather and other extraneous factors.

Case CF-2

Johnny Jones, controller for Nielsen Manufacturing, maintains that the financial statements of Nielsen should be organized and prepared such that the information is presented in a way that it is most useful to Nielsen Manufacturing. Sharon Smith, the Treasurer of Nielsen, disagrees. She believes that the approach Nielsen should take be based upon measurement certainty. Are both correct?

Case CF-3

Lynn Knapp is the new accountant for Kaag Enterprises. Kaag Enterprises consists of an automobile refinishing plant, a race car painting service company, and a custom motorcycle design and building service. They house all operations of these three activities within the automobile refinishing plant. Due to liability issues, each of these are separate legal entities. Can they combine them for financial reporting purposes?

REVENUE RECOGNITION

Case RR-1

Green Prince, a cannery specializing in no-chemical vegetables, sold most of its inventory of canned green beans to Hardy Holdings. Green Prince expects to repurchase the inventory as it needs to fulfill customers' orders and has entered a repurchase agreement. The repurchase agreement specifies that it will negotiate the price to be paid at the time of the repurchase.

Case RR-2

Great Mowers manufactures lawn mowers for sale to major hardware and home repair chains. Great Mowers sells these mowers to seven different hardware and home repair store chains. These sales contain a ninety-day right of return but Great Mowers has never received any mowers back since it started in 1983. In addition, Great Mowers guarantees to undertake an extensive $1,000,000 national advertising campaign to promote the high quality and dependability of the lawn mowers.

Case RR-3

Kate Smith, the chief accountant for LADDI Enterprises, is investigating various methods for recognizing profits on long-term construction contracts. Ms. Smith recalls learning only two methods in school—completed contract and percentage-of-completion. She is particularly interested in determining whether methods other than the cost-to-cost method are allowed in practice.

Case RR-4

BIG BEANS, a multi-state soybean operation in Iowa, Illinois, Kansas, and Missouri, just completed harvesting 4,000,000 bushels of beans. Of this total, it immediately sold and transferred 1,000,000 bushels to grain elevators at a price of $18.00 per bushel. It has sold another 500,000 bushels for delivery within the next two months at $17.75 per bushel. Although not yet sold, it recorded revenue of $17.75 (the current market price) per bushel for the remaining bushels of beans.

Case RR-5

Sinns Electric sold an office building and retail store to Iroquois State Savings & Loan Association for a total contract price of $675,000. The details of the sales agreement required a nonrefundable $25,000 down payment with the balance due in twenty monthly installments. A finance charge of 8% per year is to also be included in the payments. At the time of the sale, Sinns Electric treated this transaction as an installment sale.

Case RR-6

Gulbransen Services sold a parcel of twenty acres to Allison Racing Products for use as a potential building site. The sales agreement required Allison Racing Products to provide a deposit of $5,000 with a balance of $95,000 due within one year. Allison Racing Products is depending upon two major wins by its racing team to provide the cash needed to consummate the purchase. If Allison fails to complete the purchase within the specified one-year period, the deposit is not refundable and Gulbransen can proceed to market the parcel to other interested parties.

Case RR-7

Gossett Company signed an agreement with Hamilton Products to purchase 100 acres of land as a potential building site. As part of the agreement, the land is to remain in Hamilton Products' possession and Hamilton is responsible for maintenance. Gossett Company can request transfer of the title to the land anytime. If Gossett Company fails to request transfer within two years, the property reverts to Hamilton and Gossett will receive the purchase price less a reasonable fee to cover any maintenance or related expenses incurred by Hamilton Products.

OVERVIEW OF FINANCIAL STATEMENTS–INCOME, FINANCIAL POSITION, AND CASH FLOWS

Case OFS-1

Klaber Company transports grain on the Mississippi River using barges and tugboats. In the normal course of business it expects that once every year or two a load of grain may be lost due to a barge mishap. When these mishaps occur, the accountant for Klaber Company records the total cost of the grain as an expense of the period in which the mishap occurs.

Case OFS-2

Cozaic, an Internet software development company, produces software of two types. One type of software delivers video via the Internet. The other software consists of network administration tools. Cozaic has sold all of the network administration software to another company with the intention of focusing solely on video delivery applications. Total revenues from the software sales have been split approximately even over the past few years. The controller for Cozaic plans to report the sale of the network administration software as a disposal of a segment of the business on the current year's statement of income.

Case OFS-3

Smith Glass Company sells glass products in the wholesale market through the United States and has offices in forty-two states. One of its most profitable items is replacement sliding glass doors. Until recently, Smith Glass had a very large inventory of untempered glass doors. Recent federal legislation made these doors obsolete since tempered glass is now required for all sliding glass doors. Fortunately, Smith Glass sold the untempered doors to a retail home improvement chain in Mexico. However, the loss on the doors is $4,500,000, and Smith Glass will report it as an extraordinary item on this year's income statement.

Case OFS-4

Carlson Company has extinguished some of its debt in each of the last five years. For the most recent year, the extinguishment has resulted in a loss while a gain resulted in all of the prior years. Although it has reported these transactions as extraordinary items on the income statement, the new controller questions the propriety of reporting this year's loss as extraordinary. The controller doubts that one can consider this year's extinguishment as extraordinary since extinguishments have occurred in each of the last five years.

Case OFS-5

Gholson Corporation recently changed from the straight-line depreciation method to the double-declining-balance depreciation method. It reported the cumulative effect as an increase in the current year's depreciation expense of $5,000,000.

Case OFS-6

Eastern Illinois Power Company operates a nuclear power plant in Gore, Illinois, as well as coal- and gas-powered plants in Danville and Decatur. The normal investment in nuclear fuel rods is about $100 million at any given time with inventories of coal and gas averaging around $18 million. Once the reactor in the nuclear power plant is operating in a steady state, the company replaces one third of the fuel rods in the core every eighteen months. Currently, the fuel rods and the gas and coal inventories are aggregated and reported as fuel inventory on the statement of financial position.

Case OFS-7

Peterson Corporation currently has investments in debt securities with a historical cost of $456,000. Of this amount, $400,000 (current fair market value of $410,000) represents securities that Peterson Corporation expects to hold until maturity. The remaining $56,000 are bonds of Jayco Corporation that Peterson expects will continue to rise in price. Currently, these bonds have a fair market value of $65,000 and Peterson Corporation plans to sell them when the fair market value reaches $70,000. What is the appropriate classification for these securities on Peterson Corporation's statement of financial position?

Case OFS-8

G. Dean & Company currently has a $250,000 short-term loan from the Champaign Bank. The loan is due on January 22, 1998. However, G. Dean & Company plans to sell $250,000 worth of ten-year bonds to refinance the loan. Jay Smith, a prominent business owner in the community, has expressed an interest in purchasing the bonds. Accordingly, G. Dean & Company will report the short-term loan on its December 31, 1997, statement of financial position as a noncurrent liability.

Case OFS-9

Corkindale Company has always had a policy of taking aggressive positions regarding its federal income tax liability. This has resulted in several contested amounts and the Internal Revenue Service is currently challenging Corkindale. The IRS is challenging all of the prior three years' tax returns and three different court cases are pending. To avoid any potential penalties, Corkindale has paid the contested deficiencies to the IRS and is litigating for recovery. Corkindale's tax counsel maintains that the probability of prevailing is almost certain.

Case OFS-10

In preparing the first set of financial statements for Glasgo Company, Luke Skyrighter prepared the following note to the financial statements:

> Accounting methods are very difficult to understand and differences between them are confusing even for most accountants. Accordingly, so as not to confuse the reader of these financial statements, significant accounting policies and procedures are not discussed. All methods chosen are consistent with generally accepted accounting principles and are conservative. Some methods employed are industry specific.

Case OFS-11

Bill Smith, the accountant for TriMAX Enterprises, maintains that the company's statement of cash flows should be very simple since it should have only cash inflows and outflows from operating activities. Bill maintains that all activities of the company are related to the production of income and therefore should be considered operating activities. Bill's argument confuses Sharon Kerns, the recently hired controller. She knows that TriMAX has recently purchased and sold fixed assets and recently borrowed money from the local bank. She agrees that these activities have some effects on income–for instance, depreciation on the fixed assets or the interest expense on the bank borrowings.

CASH AND RECEIVABLES

Case CR-1

Delmar Corporation is required by its major raw materials supplier (Brazilian Jungle Products) to maintain a minimum balance of $1,000,000 in the First Brazil National Bank in San Paulo, Brazil. Brazilian Jungle Products requires the payments for its sales of raw materials to Delmar to be paid through this account and that the balance must be maintained daily. Failure to maintain the minimum balance would result in an immediate shutdown of all raw material transports and would significantly disrupt the production of Delmar. The controller of Delmar Corporation maintains that it should include the cash balance in First Brazil National Bank in the general cash account on Delmar's financial statements.

Case CR-2

The Rinadale Company manufactures and sells very high-quality men's business suits to major department store chains. To stimulate sales, Rinadale Company offered all new first-time customers a special deal. New customers could purchase up to $100,000 of suits using an open credit line. If the purchaser continues to make timely payments on any subsequent purchases, Rinadale Company defers the original purchase payment due date. If the purchaser fails to make additional purchases within sixty days or timely payments, the amount of the original purchase is immediately due along with interest of the prime rate plus 2.5% from the date of the original sale.

Case CR-3

Luce Bruce Company has recently started a business selling dormitory-sized refrigerators to students at many major colleges and universities. Students purchase the refrigerators for either $100 cash or $30 down and three installments of $30 due at the end of the next three months. Only about 25% of the sales are at the cash price with most students preferring to spread out the payments. Sally Rogers, the accountant for Luce Bruce, maintains that some accounts will turn out to be uncollectible and that an allowance for Uncollectables must be determined and Luce Bruce must recognize the accompanying bad debt expense although it has no experience with sales on account to students. Is Sally correct?

Case CR-4

Drollinger, Incorporated exchanged a 2% five-year $10,000 note for a long-term productive asset. The productive asset is a stamping press that should have a ten-year life with a salvage value of about $800. The fair market value of the stamping press at the time of the exchange was $8,000.

Case CR-5

Carpet City sells a significant amount of its carpet on a same-as-cash-basis. The terms are usually zero down payment and twenty-four months of payments. No interest is imputed if the customer makes the monthly payments and pays off the balance at the end of the twenty-four months. Since Carpet City requires cash to support its operations, it usually sells these receivables to Buyers Finance, Incorporated. All risks of collection are transferred to Buyers Finance. However, if more than 60% of the receivables are paid promptly (within the twenty- four-month schedule) with no additional interest accrued, Buyers Finance has the right to collect a finance fee of 10% of the total loan amount.

Case CR-6

Drollinger's Department Stores, a locally owned and operated department store in Mahomet, Illinois, extends very favorable credit terms to local customers to gain their loyalty to shopping locally. This is very important to Drollinger's business since there are several discount stores in a neighboring city that carry much of the same merchandise. Many customers at Drollinger's work at the local grain processing plant. Unfortunately, full employment at the local grain mill depends upon grain prices, as well as local and regional weather. The grain mill employees are unionized and have a history of strikes–the current contract expires next month.

INVENTORY AND COST OF GOODS SOLD

Case INV-1

Aces Hardwares and Building Supplies, a national chain of retail home remodeling stores, manufacturers its own paint in a facility near Chicago, Illinois. The paint manufacturing facility also manufactures paint that it sells to other chain stores and other markets. To help in solving its cash flow problems, Aces sells all of its current paint inventory to Windy City Holdings under a repurchase agreement. Under this repurchase agreement, Aces is required to repurchase the paint (as needed) from Windy City at a price that covers (1) the original sales price, (2) all holding costs incurred by Windy City, and (3) a return of 1% per month.

Case INV-2

Rambo Records has initiated a program in which it sends out "expected" hit CDs on a unique approval basis. The purchaser is entitled to return the CD anytime if the CD fails to make the "top 100" hit list. This is a new program and Rambo Records has no experience with this sort of a marketing scheme. Recently, Rambo Records sent out 10,000 CDs under this new program and billed customers $14.99 per CD plus shipping.

Case INV-3

Jenny Smith, the new controller for Burton Manufacturing, recalls, "There seems to be some requirement somewhere in the accounting professional pronouncements that the inventory cost flow must portray the actual flow of goods–if not, the most conservative method is then appropriate." If Ms. Smith is correct, Burton Manufacturing must spend a significant amount of effort, time, and money determining exactly the physical flow of its inventory.

Case INV-4

Culbert's Custom Manufacturing produces three different styles of ceramic birdbaths. In reviewing the ending inventory balance for the year, Cody Smith determined that the inventory consisted of 8,000 units of the flower bath, 4,000 units of the shell bath, and 2,000 units of the acorn bath. Cody also determined that the market value of the acorn baths had fallen to the point that Culbert's might need to revalue the inventory to the lower-of-cost-or-market. Additional information revealed that the value of the total birdbath inventory was still above cost.

Case INV-5

Tobek Plumbing has entered an agreement to purchase 10,000 feet of 2-inch copper pipe during the next calendar year at a price of $1.83 per foot. Tobek will use all of the copper pipe in a hotel construction project to be completed over the next two years. It has already signed the contract for the hotel construction project. As of the end of the current reporting year, the price of 2-inch copper pipe has dropped to $1.67 per foot. Unfortunately, Tobek's purchase agreement cannot be canceled.

Case INV-6

Grain & Fibre Foods produces granola cereal for sale to large grocery store chains. As part of the production process, Grain & Fibre uses large quantities of corn, oats, wheat, and soybeans. To induce local production of these grains, Grain & Fibre contracts with more than 300 farmers to purchase their crops at a set price with a set delivery. A buyer representative of Grain & Fibre negotiates each price with the farmer. To offset the potential swings in prices and to reduce the risk of paying a higher than market price for the grain at the time of delivery, Grain & Fibre enters several futures contracts as hedges. At the end of the year, Grain & Fibre has grain inventories, purchase commitments, and some forward contracts (being used as hedges) outstanding.

PROPERTY, PLANT, AND EQUIPMENT AND COST AMORTIZATION

Case PPE-1

Illinois Canning Company is constructing a new cannery and warehouse facility. The company plans to capitalize interest during the two-year construction project. It started the project last year and the warehouse component was completed within three months. Capitalization of interest continues on the warehouse although Illinois Canning has rented it out to other businesses until the cannery is completed.

Case PPE-2

Bionic Equipment, a manufacturer of exercise equipment, traded a warehouse located in Lexington, Kentucky, for a warehouse in Fargo, North Dakota, and owned by Smith Home Products. The Lexington warehouse had a market value of $4,500,000 and a book value of $1,900,000 while the Fargo facility had a book value of $2,800,000 and a market value of $4,000,000. Smith Home Products also paid Bionic $300,000.

Case PPE-3

Glover Enterprises received a donation of 100 acres from the city of New Orleans as an incentive for Glover to locate a new plant in New Orleans. The grant stipulates that Glover Enterprises must build a manufacturing plant and a warehouse containing at least 250,000 square feet. In addition, at least 20 acres must be used as a parking lot. All construction must be completed within three years. At the time of the donation, the fair market value of the tract of land was $2,200,000. On December 31, the year-end date for Glover Enterprises, the fair market value of the land had fallen to $2,000,000 and no construction had yet begun.

Case PPE-4

ESSON's oil refinery in North Korea was expropriated by the government last week due to a disagreement over the control of sales to other foreign countries. ESSON received $45,000,000 from the government for the refinery that had a book value of $23,000,000 and an estimated fair market value of $42,000,000.

Case PPE-5

High on the Hog Company operates large swine feedlots in Iowa, Illinois, and Missouri. The company planned to expand its operations and purchased 160 acres near Rankin, Illinois, on which to build a new large-scale swine lot. The cost of the acreage was $618,000 and construction costs of $234,000 had been incurred when it scrapped the project. Due to negative public sentiment and the high probability that new state laws would be enacted to prohibit operating the lot, High on the Hog Company sold the facility for $580,000.

Case PPE-6

Northern Utah Electric Company operates a nuclear power plant as well as four coal-fired power generating stations. Due to operating difficulties, the Nuclear Regulatory Commission shut down the nuclear reactor two years ago and has not allowed it to operate since. Although Northern Utah Electric is optimistic it will be able to operate the nuclear power plant in the future, there is some possibility it will never operate again.

Case PPE-7

Four years ago, Deep Black Coal Company wrote down the carrying value of its mine as an asset impairment. This action was prompted by state legislation that reduced the amount of pollutants that the local electric company could emit. Rather than investing in scrubbers to clean the smoke, the local electric utility switched to natural gas for electricity generation. The write-down reduced the carrying value of the mine from $22,000,000 to $2,000,000. Recently, Deep Black Coal Company has considered selling the mine to Kentucky Nuclear Waste Management Corporation as a storage location for nuclear wastes. An appraisal of the mine as a nuclear waste storage location suggests its market value to be no less than $10,000,000.

Case PPE-8

In reviewing the financial statements of Taylor Manufacturing Company, you discover that the financial statements portray only the net amount of property, plant, and equipment with no information about the balance in accumulated depreciation. However, the supplemental notes to the financial statements do provide information regarding the current period depreciation expense and the method used to compute depreciation.

Case PPE-9

Capital Oil Exploration uses the full-cost method of accounting for its petroleum exploration activities. As of the current year-end, the balance in the capitalized costs is $36,000,000. The amount of proven oil reserves that this represents is about one million barrels. The current market price is $34 per barrel. Capital Oil expects that it will pump and sell these reserves within the next twelve months at a price of at least $37 per barrel. Capital Oil is confident that the price of oil will rise significantly in the next few months.

Case PPE-10

Wildcatter Smith Company, a small oil and gas exploration and production company, uses full-costing to account for its exploration activities. The current book value of these assets is $43,000,000. Other than including a line item on the statement of financial position for these assets, it provides no other disclosures.

INVESTMENTS

Case INVEST-1

To simplify its financial statements, AGRI TECH aggregates its accounts receivables into bundles by maturity period and considers them an investment. These bundles of receivables represent future cash flows consisting of both principal and interest. The controller of AGRI TECH believes that this approach is appropriate since AGRI TECH has sold several receivable bundles to financial institutions for cash. In fact, previously AGRI TECH has sold receivable bundles and then subsequently repurchased them just a few weeks later.

Case INVEST-2

Alonzo Incorporated does not carry at current market value its investments in marketable securities that it classifies as trading. This decision is based on the fact that the investments are in securities that are traded only on the Taiwan stock exchange.

Case INVEST-3

Arnolds Corporation holds twenty two percent of the outstanding shares of Smith-Benny Incorporated and accounts for the investment using the equity method. Recently, Arnolds Corporation failed to get a representative from Arnolds Corporation elected to the board of directors of Smith-Benny.

Case INVEST-4

DU-ALL Furniture recently recorded an impairment in the value of its debt security investments in Ellis Insurance because of the financial difficulty Ellis was experiencing. After writing down the investment to its market value, DU-ALL plans to amortize the original discount on the bonds over ten years rather than the remaining fifteen years of the bonds' life.

INTANGIBLES

Case INT-1

Unger Corporation amortizes its intangible assets over their expected useful lives. On average, Unger Corporation uses a fifteen-year life. Fifteen years is considered appropriate since Unger Corporation computes it as the average life of all of the intangibles with determinable lives. Unger Corporation does not include intangibles with indeterminable lives in the amortization computation.

Case INT-2

Wolfe Enterprises, a new start-up company, will build custom personal computers. Wolfe Enterprises has been preparing to start operating for the past six months and is almost ready to start production. It has incurred significant costs but no revenue has yet to be earned. Organization costs such as legal fees and advertising have been capitalized as start-up costs. Wolfe Enterprises has expensed all payroll expenses, rent, and other similar costs–this has resulted in a significant loss being reported on the first year's financial statements.

Case INT-3

Quick Express Packing is a national chain of franchises that prepares packages for shipping via the United Package Service. Each local franchisee pays significant franchise fees for assistance in setting up the business and for the priority access to United Package Service services. In the Chicago area, Desmond Enterprises owns fifteen Quick Express Packing franchises with a capitalized value of $13,000,000 on its books. Due to recent strikes by the employees of United Package Service and the high likelihood of more employee strikes in the future, many regular customers of Quick Express Packing have shifted to other carriers.

Case INT-4

Janet Smith, a lawyer and certified public accountant employed by Kisso and Willis, specializes in providing expert witness testimony and litigation support services. Recently, Janet has been asked to provide expert witness testimony regarding the use of the master valuation approach to computing goodwill. Janet needs a listing of citations in which "master valuation" approaches are discussed in the professional accounting literature as well as a brief description of the accepted approaches for computing goodwill.

Case INT-5

Young TV Supply recently purchased Yergler Electronic Supplies for $2,500,000 cash. At the time of acquisition, the net current assets of Yergler were worth $800,000 while the net noncurrent assets were worth $2,100,000. Young recorded both the net current assets and net noncurrent assets at their fair market values.

Case INT-6

Sam's Appliances entered a long-term lease agreement with Smith Properties. Sam's Appliances made significant improvements to the store being leased and capitalized these improvements. Recently, changes in traffic patterns and a higher incidence of crime in the area have resulted in a very significant decline in the number of customers. This decline is substantial and has resulted in Sam's Appliances converting the store to a warehouse facility. The current amounts of the capitalized leasehold and the improvements are $120,000 and $22,000, respectively. Sam's Appliances estimates that it would cost about $140,000 to lease warehouse space equivalent to the recently converted store for the period of the lease.

Case INT-7

Garner & Garner is a manufacturing company that started its own research and development department this past year. Significant effort was involved in setting up the R&D facilities. Accordingly, Garner & Garner has expensed all general and administrative costs of its current period as research and development expenses.

Case INT-8

Campbell Company, as a part of its business, researches and develops pharmaceutical products related to blood disorders. As part of that research, Campbell Company has entered a contract with Majek Corporation to analyze particular substances that are of commercial interest to Majek. The process of analyzing these substances is usually secondary to Campbell Company's main projects. Campbell Company performs these services throughout the year and then bills Majek at the end of each quarter on a cost plus basis. Campbell Company's accounting policy is to expense all research and development costs, including those costs related to the Majek projects.

Case INT-9

VIDEOZAIC designs, develops, and markets computer software for streaming video images on the Internet. Although no working prototype has yet been developed, the software designers and developers at VIDEOZAIC are confident that a product will be available commercially within a few more months. Besides its own development activities, VIDEOZAIC purchased the rights to a video enhancement program that is an integral part of the video streaming software. Given its specifications, the video enhancement program could be used in other software applications. Another major cost has been the hiring of an internationally famous patent attorney to help in obtaining the patents for the software components and to insure that competitors, who are developing similar products, do not infringe upon VIDEOZAIC's rights. They are currently capitalizing these costs.

CURRENT LIABILITIES AND CONTINGENCIES

Case CL-1

Smith Brothers' financial statements currently show $350,000 of current liabilities. Of this amount, $200,000 represents a liability to Bishop Manufacturing. This obligation is expected to be liquidated by transferring three patents held by Smith Brothers to Bishop Manufacturing. The three patents have a book value of only $1.00 but have a fair market value of approximately $190,000.

Case CL-2

James Smith, a recent accounting graduate, has just started working for Grant Ross & Company, an importer of single malt scotch whiskey. Grant Ross purchases single malt scotch whiskey in Scotland, transports it to its warehouse in New Orleans, Louisiana, and stores it for up to twenty years in charred oaken casks. None of the whiskey is ever sold until after it has aged at least twelve years. To finance expansion, Grant Ross recently sold $2,500,000 of ten-year bonds. Smith believes that Grant Ross should classify the bonds as long-term debt but is not completely sure.

Case CL-3

Bauer Farm Services is expecting to refinance $10,000,000 of short-term notes. It currently classifies the notes as current liabilities. Bauer Farm Services has applied to the Cissna Bank for a five-year $8,000,000 loan, but as of today, the end of the accounting year, Bauer Farm Services and the bank continue to negotiate collateral requirements.

Case CL-4

Beck and Solomon, a farm equipment manufacturer, has arranged to refinance the currently due portion of its long-term debt by issuing a new class of equity shares to the creditor. Although it has not yet issued the securities, an irrevocable agreement exists between Beck and Solomon and the creditor. The accountant for Beck and Solomon plans to include a footnote in the financial statements that includes a very brief description of the agreement.

Case CL-5

All employees of Doupak Corporation are entitled to take four personal leave days each year. Employees earn this benefit upon completing one week of employment and can accumulate the personal days until they actually take them. Any employee leaving the company receives a check for the accumulated days based upon the wage rate at the time of termination. Since Doupak Company does not believe it can reasonably estimate the amount to be paid, it provides no accrual or disclosure in the financial statements.

Case CL-6

In preparing the current year's financial statements, Annie Peters realizes that the accounts payables owed to suppliers are not valued at present value. Upon closer scrutiny, Annie determines that a significant amount of the payables is not due to transactions arising in the normal course of business but is related to special financing arrangements.

Case CL-7

AUTO-ADVANTAGE sells used automobiles released by the major rental companies through a network of fifty auto superstores. As an incentive to purchasers, each automobile comes with a security system with a lucrative guarantee–if the car is stolen, and the purchaser's insurance fails to cover the cost of the auto (less the deductible), AUTO-ADVANTAGE will replace the auto. To qualify for the program, the purchaser must carry theft insurance on the automobile with a deductible of no more than $50. Since its inception three years ago, only one claim has been submitted and it occurred within the last two days.

Case CL-8

The state environmental protection agency assessed Bloomington Production a significant fine for effluent discharges that significantly polluted a local stream. In addition to the fine, the state environmental protection agency required Bloomington Production to pay for cleanup costs. The total amounted to $250,000, and Bloomington Production has already paid the state and recorded a loss. Subsequently, Bloomington Production submitted a claim to its insurance company and maintained that the discharge was due to an accident that its insurance covers. On its financial statements, Bloomington Production offset the loss against the expected insurance proceeds and reported a net loss equal to the insurance deductible.

Case CL-9

Until recently, Birkey's Farm Store has been paying $1,200 per month for fire insurance coverage on its repair garage. After experiencing some cash flow difficulties, the management of Birkey's decided to drop the fire insurance and to be self-insured. Each month the bookkeeper records insurance expense of $1,200 and credits "Expected Liability Under Self-Insurance."

LONG-TERM LIABILITIES

Case LTL-1

Burton Motors recently issued $100,000 of ten-year six percent bonds and received $98,600 from the proceeds of the sale. In addition, Burton Motors incurred $2,800 in legal fees and other costs related to the sale of the bonds. It expensed all of the issuance costs in the period of the issuance.

Case LTL-2

F.S. Heritage, Incorporated recently extinguished two of its bond issues. It extinguished both bond issues before maturity. For one of the bond issues, the Class A bonds, a gain resulted from this early extinguishment. A loss on the early extinguishment resulted for the other (Class B) bonds. Since F.S. Heritage had previously extinguished some of its Class A bonds, it treated the gain as an ordinary gain. It treated the loss on the Class B bonds as an extraordinary loss since no Class B bonds had ever been extinguished before.

Case LTL-3

Gleason Company, a local retail department store chain, and Abby Smythe Incorporated, a long-distance trucking firm, entered an interest rate swap agreement. Gleason swapped the interest payments on its $100,000 fixed rate loan from the Dansville Bank for Smythe's floating rate interest payments on its $100,000 variable rate line of credit from First Rank Bank of Cheneyville. Gleason fixed rate loan is at 8% and matures in five years. Smythe's floating rate line of credit requires interest payments of prime rate plus 2.25%. The prime rate of interest at the time of the swap was 5.75%. As part of the swap agreement, both Gleason and Smythe will continue to make the payments on their own loans and will then settle up any changes in interest rates at the end of Gleason's five-year loan. Since both organizations are continuing to pay their own interest payments, they provided no disclosure of the swap in either entity's financial statements. The controller for Gleason based this on the fact that there had been not any change in the prime rate since they began the swap agreement.

Case LTL-4

McMurray Bicycle Company has approximately $10,000,000 of long-term debt outstanding. About $1,000,000 is due each of the next five years with $5,000,000 due in seven years. McMurray shows the debt on its financial statements at its present value with a footnote disclosure of the face value and the effective interest rate.

Case LTL-5

To guarantee a continuous supply of coal at its electricity generating plant in Marion, Kentucky, General Power persuaded Kentucky Coal to build a coal mine next to the power plant. As part of the agreement, General Power will unconditionally purchase all of the coal production from the mine for the next ten years. The agreed-upon price is the current market price at the time Kentucky Coal transfers the coal to the generating plant plus $.04 per ton. Betty Lane, an auditor for Lane & Smith, is auditing General Power's financial statements. Ms. Lane is concerned that General Power has entered a contract that is economically equivalent to a futures contract and must account for it as a financial instrument.

Case LTL-6

Wendy Smith, an auditor for Smith & Smith, helps in the audit of both the First Bank of Rantoul and Bull Helmets. Ms. Smith is disturbed that a recent trouble debt restructuring between the First Bank of Rantoul and Bull Helmets resulted in First Bank reporting a loss while Bull Helmets recorded no gain. Ms. Smith does not understand how the same transaction could result in such a difference in the way they treat it for financial accounting purposes.

INCOME TAXES

Case IT-1

In preparing its financial statements for the past year, Lobers Incorporated recognized a deferred tax asset due to some timing differences related to environmental cleanup costs. Stan Smith, the accountant for Lobers, has projected that it is reasonably likely (about 50%) that Lobers will not be able to recognize the cleanup costs on its future tax returns due to expected changes in the tax law.

Case IT-2

As an incentive to get Robust Manufacturing to locate near Indianapolis, the county provided a potential moratorium on property taxes for Robust Manufacturing. The incentive agreement requires Robust to pay property taxes on all real estate but to be able to apply for a refund of those property taxes if the company is employing more than 1,000 people within the next three years. Robust Manufacturing reports the real estate taxes as an expense on both its financial statements and its federal income tax return but recognizes a deferred tax asset arising from the expected refund of the property in the next year or so.

Case IT-3

In its most current set of financial statements, Nielsen Company reports a deferred tax liability of $500,000 due to a temporary difference. Subsequently, Congress has passed a new tax bill that has been signed into effect raising the corporate income tax rate from 28% to 38%.

Case IT-4

Prairieview Company reports a deferred tax asset on its latest set of financial statements. Recently, the company has decided to revise its policies regarding the aggressiveness of its income tax strategies. Due to recent tax court decisions against Prairieview, the company has decided to be much less aggressive.

PENSIONS AND OTHER POST-EMPLOYMENT BENEFITS

Case POPEB-1

The employees of Rural Health Products participate in a defined contribution pension plan. Until the current year, Rural Health Products contributed 8% of the employee's salary as an employment benefit. However, due to recent cash flow problems, Rural Health Products has reduced its contribution to 4%. Accordingly, it will report a lower pension expense for the period. To reduce negative publicity, no other disclosures about the pension plan will be provided in the financial statements.

Case POPEB-2

Gibson Enterprises sponsors two different defined benefit pension plans for its employees. Each plan is separate and cannot be used to pay benefits to participants in the other plan. For all financial reporting purposes, Gibson Enterprises combines the two plans and nets the amounts together.

Case POPEB-3

James Schlitz Company recently (this year) amended its defined benefit pension plan to provide an increase in benefits to its employees. In line with conservatism, it recognized the total cost of this amendment as pension expense in the current year statement of income.

Case POPEB-4

General Automobile Manufacturing (GAM) participates along with several other motor vehicle production companies in a multi-employer pension plan for its employees. In its financial statements, GAM reports only the amount of cash contributed to the plan as a current period expense.

Case POPEB-5

TERRA Company terminated its defined benefit pension plan by providing a cash settlement to all of its participants. The total cost of the settlement was $45,000,000 while the reported pension liability on the financial statements was $42,000,000. It has accrued the difference between the recorded liability and the settlement, and will amortize it over the remaining service lives of the employees.

Case POPEB-6

Upon adoption of the financial accounting and reporting requirements for other post-employment benefits other than pensions, Woodland Fire Alarm Company commenced amortizing its transition obligation using a very unique approach. Woodland Fire Alarm Company divided the total transition obligation by its number of employees. It recognizes an amount equal to this transition obligation per employee as an expense when the employee leaves or retires.

LEASES

Case LEASE-1

Northern Michigan Power leases the fuel rods for its nuclear power plant. The lease agreement does not contain a bargain purchase option or transfer ownership. In addition, Northern Michigan Power leases the fuel rods for half their economically productive life. A component of the lease payments (40%) includes a charge for storage of the depleted rods and the costs of operating a nuclear waste facility by the lessor. Northern Michigan Power capitalizes the nuclear fuel rod leases since the present value of the lease payments equals 92% of the fair market value of the fuel rods.

Case LEASE-2

John Smith Corporation has agreed to enter a noncancellable lease arrangement. However, the actual lease will not commence until three years from now. John Smith Corporation wanted to lock-in the lease cost since they expect that the supply of the leased asset will be limited in the future when they will actually use the asset for production. Under the terms of the agreement, the leased asset will be shipped to John Smith Corporation in about thirty months and lease payments will commence three months after the equipment is installed and operational.

Case LEASE-3

Betty Jones, the accountant for Hybrid Research Company, wishes to structure the lease on a production machine so that it will not meet the criteria for capitalization. She can structure the lease so that it will not meet the transfer of ownership test, the bargain purchase option test, and the economic life test. However, given that the lessor requires the residual to be guaranteed, the present value of the minimum lease payments meets the recovery of investment test for capitalization. How might Betty structure the lease so that it fails the investment test but continues to have the same lease payments and the guaranteed residual?

Case LEASE-4

Yergler Companies, the lessor, incurred $10,000 of origination fees associated with the leasing of three production machines to Molly's Cement Products. Yergler treated the lease as a direct financing lease and recorded the origination fees as an expense of the period in which it signed the lease agreement.

Case LEASE-5

Park Television Sales entered a sale and leaseback arrangement in which it sold a warehouse to Knapps Shoe Supply for $150,000 and arranged to lease it back for three months at $2,000 per month. The book value of the warehouse was $48,000 and Park Television Sales deferred the recognition of the gain on the sale with the intent of amortizing it over the remaining life of the warehouse–twelve years.

CONTRIBUTED CAPITAL

Case CC-1

MacIntyre Machinery, a company that builds custom conveyor equipment, repurchased some of its own stock and accounted for the transaction using the cost method. The subsequent sale of some of the treasury stock at a price much less than the purchase price resulted in MacIntyre recording a negative balance in additional paid-in capital.

Case CC-2

General Construction Corporation recently acquired some of its own shares. Since the company intends to retire the shares within the next few weeks, the cost method was used to record the treasury stock acquisition.

Case CC-3

Natbard Plumbing Fixtures has $10,000,000 of $4.00 par value, redeemable preferred stock aggregated with its common stock on its statement of financial position. The preferred stock is redeemable at a price of $4.50 per share.

Case CC-4

Gleason Manufacturing received land valued at $2,500,000 from the City of Decatur as an incentive to locate a new plant in Decatur. The contribution agreement stipulates that Gleason must start building the new plant within eighteen months. Failure to start construction would result in Gleason having either to purchase the land or to return it to the city. To obtain some necessary cash to begin construction of the new plant, Gleason used the land as collateral for a loan from the United Bank of Decatur.

RETAINED EARNINGS

Case RE-1

Parkway Enterprises has determined that it will liquidate one of its major businesses (home repair and remodeling services) by paying the current stockholders a property dividend. All the tools and equipment used for the home repair and remodeling services will be distributed to the current common stockholders. They will distribute the dividend based upon the equipment's fair market value and the stockholders' proportionate shares of the common stock.

Case RE-2

Due to the likelihood that a lawsuit would be filed regarding the safety of one of its products, Weber Industries appropriated $1,000,000 of retained earnings by recording a contingent liability.

Case RE-3

Travel Discoveries Incorporated arranges and provides bus tours for elderly customers. These tours may be as short as a few hours to more than two weeks. Because of some cash flow difficulties, Travel Discoveries reduced the amount of its liability insurance coverage from $10,000,000 to $2,500,000 and saved $1,200 per month in premiums. Given that Travel Discoveries is self-insuring itself for the difference ($7,500,000) and wants to be conservative in its financial statements, it records $1,200 each month as a reduction of retained earnings and an increase in contingent liabilities.

Case RE-4

Buddy Young Company has a complex capital structure. It consists of a single class of common stock and two classes of preferred stock. For all financial reporting, it combines the three classes of equity.

EPS AND DILUTIVE SECURITIES

Case EPS-1

Woodland Alarm Manufacturing has recently converted some of its convertible debt to equity. To induce the bondholders to convert, Woodland offered a "kicker" of 1% of the face value of the debt in cash. Although there was a difference between the fair market values of the debt and equity in the conversion, it recorded no gain or loss and it accounted for the "kicker" as an adjustment to the equity issued.

Case EPS-2

Yergler Jewelry Manufacturing offers its employees a nonqualified stock option plan in which employees can purchase shares of stock for a discount from the current market price. The amount of the discount is equal to the number of years the employee has worked for Yergler times .25%. A worker with ten years at Yergler would get a discount of 2.5% while a worker with forty years would get 10%. Yergler defers the recognition of the expense and amortizes it over the lesser of the expected remaining period it will employ the employee or ten years.

ACCOUNTING CHANGES

Case AC-1

Henning's Beer Company recently changed from the LIFO inventory method to FIFO so as to more closely approximate the physical flow of its production. Henning's Beer Company treated the cumulative effect of this change in accounting principle as a one-time adjustment to cost of goods sold in the current period financial statements.

Case AC-2

It has been Jackson Recreational Transport Company's accounting policy to defer triennial state licensing fees for its ferries and passenger transport boats and then to amortize them over the following three years on a straight-line basis. Based upon experiences with irregular schedules for the ferries and passenger boats, Jackson Recreational Transport Company revised its policy to immediately expense the licensing fees in the period paid. Jackson Recreational Transport Company treated the change as a change in accounting estimate.

FULL DISCLOSURE

Case FD-1

For determining if a segmental disclosure is required, Russel Leigh Company has always assumed that firms are constrained to report no more than five segments. In an analysis of its segments, Russel Leigh Company determined that it has at least six segments that meet the criteria for being reported. However, it will report only the five largest segments so as to stay within the constraint.

Case FD-2

Dilks and Rodeen Corporation has been reporting two reportable segments in its financial statements. Recently (before year-end), its management took the company private in a leverage buyout. The company is starting to prepare its financial statements for the most current year, and questions have arisen regarding the reporting of segmental information.

Case FD-3

Hamilton Manufacturing switched from a straight-line method of depreciation to a double-declining balance approach during the third quarter of the current year. In preparing its financial statements for the third quarter, it recognized the effect of the switch as an adjustment to cost of goods sold in the third quarter.

STATEMENT OF CASH FLOWS

Case SCF-1

Hines Automotive Services purchased $1,000,000 of air-conditioner freon before its distribution was banned in the United States. Hines intends to use some of the freon in its automobile air-conditioning repair business and is speculating that the price will rise significantly as supplies of the freon diminish. Hines plans to keep the remainder of the freon for speculation purposes until it at least quadruples in price. In preparing its statement of cash flows, Hines classifies the total purchase of freon as an operating activity.

Case SCF-2

First Kankakee Bank purchased $10,000,000 of loans and collateralized securities from the Grant Savings and Loan Company. First Kankakee holds the loans and securities with the intent of possibly reselling them. In its statement of cash flows, First Kankakee classified this purchase as an investing activity.

Case SCF-3

John Jones Company uses the indirect method of preparing its statement of cash flows. In computing the cash flow from operations, John Jones Company aggregates the changes in inventory, accounts receivable, and accounts payable.